COFFEE MAGIC
for the
MODERN WITCH

A Practical Guide to Coffee Rituals,
Divination Readings, Magical Brews,
Latte Sigil Writing, and More

ELSIE WILD

Published by:
ULYSSES PRESS
PO Box 3440
Berkeley, CA 94703
www.ulyssespress.com

ISBN: 978-1-64604-550-1
Library of Congress Control Number: 2023938275

Printed in the United States by Versa Press
10 9 8 7 6 5 4 3 2 1

Acquisitions editor: Kierra Sondereker
Managing editor: Claire Chun
Project editor: Renee Rutledge
Editor: Scott Calamar
Front cover design: Amy King
Interior design: what!design @ whatweb.com
Artwork: from shutterstock.com—coffee cup on front cover © Artitok; pattern
    © Murhena
Layout: Winnie Liu

NOTE TO READERS: This book has been written and published strictly for
informational and educational purposes only. It is not intended to serve as
medical advice or to be any form of medical treatment. You should always consult
your physician before altering or changing any aspect of your medical treatment
and/or undertaking a diet regimen, including the guidelines as described in
this book. Do not stop or change any prescription medications without the
guidance and advice of your physician. Any use of the information in this book
is made on the reader's good judgment after consulting with his or her physician
and is the reader's sole responsibility. This book is not intended to diagnose or
treat any medical condition and is not a substitute for a physician. This book
is independently authored and published and no sponsorship or endorsement
of this book by, and no affiliation with, any trademarked brands or other
products mentioned within is claimed or suggested. All trademarks that appear
in ingredient lists and elsewhere in this book belong to their respective owners
and are used here for informational purposes only. The author and publisher
encourage readers to patronize the brands mentioned in this book.

CONTENTS

WELCOME TO THE MAGIC OF COFFEE

*C*offee has its own kind of magic.

The kind of magic that wakes you up and gets you moving, even if you would rather stay in bed. The kind of magic that helps you connect with an old friend, even when modern life keeps your schedule booked constantly. The kind of magic that enchants a first date into a spellbinding love affair. While caffeine may work like magic, coffee has a unique blend of power that is activated with each sip.

That's the magic of coffee.

In *Herbal Tea Magic for the Modern Witch,* I wrote a lot about herbalism, the practice of studying and using plants for healing and metaphysical purposes. However, while there's been a lot of tea being spilled on the magic of tea (including by yours truly), the beans haven't been spilled on coffee yet. After all, coffee is a plant that comes from nature; therefore, it has magical properties. It is often infused or mixed with different herbs and spices. There are over a billion coffee drinkers on this earth, people who willingly get in line daily for a cup every day. People who will become overjoyed when their favorite latte is back in season. Revolutions and corporations have all begun with a cup of coffee.

You can't say that's not magic.

Coffee Magic for the Modern Witch is an introduction to the enchanting power of coffee, and how to use it in our everyday life. A mixture of herbalism and kitchen witchery with a current twist. Whether you're trying to brew your own pumpkin spice latte, banishing your ex back to hell (or at least as far away from you as humanly possible), or hoping to see your future in the grounds at the bottom of your coffee cup, I have a brew, ritual, or spell for you.

You don't have to be a self-proclaimed coffee snob or an ex-barista to read or use this book. Trust me, I'm a devoted coffee enthusiast, but until very recently, if you were to ask me to use a moka pot, I would just stare at you blankly. So, start where you are. This book will go over the basics of brewing coffee and offer an overview of spices, herbs, and their magical meanings. I'll show you the difference between a latte and a cappuccino (yes, there's a difference, I promise), and offer step-by-step guides for recipes, rituals, and brews that you can modify to fit your skills and equipment set.

You'll also learn how to incorporate the magical properties of your favorite drinks and ingredients. While you may not be stirring up eyes of newts and herbs into a cauldron to brew a love potion, you can whip up a delicious mocha to attract love to your life or use latte art to bring abundance and money.

So, put a little dash of magic in that to-go cup, and let's get started.

CREATING YOUR WITCH'S TOOL KIT

Like any craft, you'll need the right tools and materials to help make your potions, perform your rituals, and cast your spells. There are many different ways to make a damn fine cup of coffee, from simple to complex. So let's start by going over the various coffee-making equipment and methods along with other types of tools you may need throughout the book.

DRIP COFFEE

Probably the most common method of making coffee, the drip-coffee method is similar to making tea, where coffee grounds are placed in a paper filter and hot water is poured over the grounds until the brewed coffee drips down into the pot or cup. You have some options when choosing a drip coffee maker:

* **Auto-Drip Coffee Maker:** This is the most common type of coffee maker found in homes and restaurants. These are relatively cheap and easy to use, as you just add the coffee filter, grounds, and water. The machine does the rest. Perfect for making several cups of coffee at once.

* **Percolator:** Before the auto-drip coffee maker was invented, there was the percolator—a coffee pot with a chamber at the bottom. Similar in appearance to a large teakettle, percolators work by moving boiling water in cycles through coffee grounds until the coffee is ready. Percolators were commonly used on the stovetop, but there are now electric percolators you can plug in.

* **Pour-Over:** Swiftly becoming popular because of its low cost and ease of use. This method uses a coffee dripper, a cone-like device in which you place your coffee filter. Place the dripper on top of your coffee cup, place your coffee grounds in the dripper, and pour hot water over the grounds. The coffee then drips down into the cup.

STEEPED COFFEE

Another method, which tea drinkers may be familiar with, is steep brewing. Steep brewing makes coffee by adding coffee grounds to hot water and waiting for the coffee to steep out. This is different from drip coffee as this usually takes a long time, though many believe that steeping your coffee creates a richer flavor. You can make steeped coffee with:

* **French Press:** A coffee-brewing method that is growing in popularity in the US is the French press, perfect for those who don't have room for a larger electric coffee maker. A French press is a cylindrical pot that has a plunger on top with a built-in filter screen. You add coffee grounds to the press, pour in boiling water, and let it steep for a few minutes. Then, press down on the plunger to force the coffee to the bottom. This is said to produce the purest form of coffee as nothing is filtered out. A French press can also be used to brew tea and to froth milk.

* **Coffee Bags:** Fun fact, coffee can be brewed like tea by simply adding the grounds into a tea bag or infuser and placing it into boiling hot water. Let it steep for several minutes before removing the bag. Perfect for making coffee in a pinch.

PRESSURE-BREWED COFFEE

As the name suggests, pressure-brewed coffee pushes coffee grounds through hot water at a very high pressure. This makes coffee quickly, and it's usually a stronger brew. Most pressure-brewed coffee is typically an espresso, but not always. Options for pressure-brewed coffee are:

- ✵ **Espresso Machine:** I'll go over what an espresso is in Chapter Two, but if you're a person who loves a good espresso, it may be worth investing in an espresso machine. Fair warning—they are usually a few hundred dollars (and that's just for a basic one). An espresso machine is different from a coffee maker as it pushes pressurized hot water through tightly packed grounds. An espresso machine also steams milk. Alternatives to this are a manual espresso machine and an AeroPress.

- ✵ **Moka Pot:** If you don't want a big machine to clutter your counter space, consider investing in a moka pot. A moka pot makes rich coffee that is very close to authentic espresso, and you don't need to plug it into anything! To use a moka pot, you add room-temperature water to the bottom chamber of the pot. Fill the middle chamber with fine ground coffee. Place the pot on the stovetop and heat on medium heat. The pot will start to create steam, forcing the water up to the coffee grounds and percolating the coffee, creating a rich brew.

- ✵ **Single-Serve Pod Machine:** For those who want to keep their coffee method as easy and quick as possible, we have the single-serve pod machine. Just add a prepacked coffee pod into the machine, add water, and press start!

BASIC TOOLS

Once you've picked out your coffee machine (or several), it's time to stock up on your magical tools and ingredients. We'll be going over this more in Chapter One, but here are a few things you should have.

* ✳ **Coffee:** It's safe to assume that you're going to need some coffee to do just about everything in this book. While certain sections, recipes, and spells may require a particular type of coffee, you can use any coffee you wish in any of its forms: coffee beans, coffee grounds, coffee pods, and even instant coffee/espresso if you need it in a pinch. Whatever works best for you.

* ✳ **Milk, Creamers, Sugar, and Syrups:** Whether you drink your coffee black like your soul or need some extra flavor to your brew, it's good to keep milk, creamers, and sugar around to make certain coffee potions, especially if they have magical attributes you want to add. In Chapter Two, we'll be crafting different brews requiring syrups and extracts for a magical and flavorful boost. You can make your own syrup or purchase some already made. It doesn't matter what you use, it's the intention you bring into it that counts.

* ✳ **Milk Frother:** We'll be making plenty of lattes, mochas, and cappuccinos throughout the book; all that requires frothing the milk. You can pick up a milk-frothing wand, or use a French press or a whisk to achieve this.

* ✳ **Saucepan:** Throughout the book (especially Chapters Two and Three), you will be mixing a lot of herbs and spices together to make syrups and you'll want to steam milk, so

it's best to have a saucepan and a heat source (stovetop, hot plate, campfire, etc.). You can also work around this by using a microwave.

* **Mugs:** Since we'll be making coffee, it's important to have some mugs around to put your coffee in. You can use any kind of mug you desire, or keep one just for witchcraft.

* **Spoon:** Already found in your kitchen, the spoon can act as a wand for most of your spells and potions. You can use an everyday spoon or pick up a spoon with a crystal at the end of the handle, typically found in any witchy supply store.

* **Latte Pen:** A latte pen is a stainless-steel pen that is used to make latte art, perfect for creating sigil art on your latte or just making some magical designs. You can purchase a latte pen at most home goods or variety stores in person or on the web, or use a wooden stick or chopstick.

* **Grimoire (Physical or Digital):** A grimoire is a book devoted to magic and witchcraft. Many witches keep a grimoire as a handy way to access spells, references, and to record divination readings and spell results. Keep a physical grimoire in a notebook to record your witchcraft journey, or use your notes app on your phone.

* **Internet Access:** As a modern witch, technology is essential to your craft as it gives you an almost unlimited amount of knowledge to help you make magic.

Chapter 1

WHAT'S IN YOUR CUP?
An Introduction to Coffee and Its Magical Ingredients

◖ ☽ ✦ ☾ ◗

In this chapter, we'll be going over the uses, history, and magical properties of various coffee-related ingredients. From the type of roast to the extra touches, every single item has its own special intention that can make or break your spell, ritual, or brew. So, treat them with care.

COFFEE

If you couldn't guess by the title of the book, the main ingredient of all the potions, spells, and recipes I present is coffee. But what are the metaphysical and health properties of those magical beans that keep us hooked?

The Magical Properties of Coffee: Coffee is associated with all four elements: Earth, where the beans come from; Fire, which roasts the beans; Water, which is poured over the grounds to create coffee; and Air, which represents the steam from a fresh, hot cup. These elements are represented in the metaphysical properties of coffee as well. Coffee is grounding (note double meaning of that word!) and is able to stabilize us in the morning and after a long day. With its cleansing and protective abilities, coffee can dispel nightmares and remove any energy blockages that keep us from our goals. Coffee boosts stamina, allowing us to focus and motivate ourselves to achieve anything. It grants us clarity to see situations with fresh eyes. Drinking coffee can help us develop closer connections with others and even allow love to blossom. It can also spark our creativity, boost our intuition, and help us get lucky by increasing our lust and our happiness. So always ask for that second cup.

The Health Properties of Coffee: While your doctor wouldn't recommend seven large mocha lattes every day, coffee has a lot of great health benefits to enchant your life. The smell of coffee (in bean form or ground up) can help relieve some symptoms of depression. Coffee can also reduce the risk of liver disease and improve cognitive function and gut health. Sipping on coffee can evoke alertness and focus, boost skin health, cure headaches, and boost sex drive. Just remember, everything in moderation.

Health Warnings: Because coffee has caffeine, please do not consume it if you have a caffeine sensitivity or are pregnant and/or breastfeeding.

DEATH BEFORE DECAF? THINK AGAIN!

Decaf coffee gets a pretty negative reputation for being a "lesser" coffee because of its perceived lack of caffeine. While decaf is short for "decaffeinated" coffee, that doesn't mean it's 100 percent caffeine free. Decaf coffee is made by steaming unroasted coffee beans. These beans are rinsed with a solvent to eliminate the caffeine, but they manage to retain about 1 percent (or 7 milligrams per 12 ounces) of the original caffeine. While this amount of caffeine may not be able to wake us up in the morning like a regular cup of coffee can, it still has a little kick.

Because decaf and regular coffee are almost completely the same, except for the amount of caffeine, the magical properties are the same. So, you can easily swap in decaf for practically all of the recipes and spells in this book. Due to the low amount of caffeine, it's not the best for spells and potions that require speed and high energy. Decaf, though, is ideal for potions and spells that call for grounding, protection, and bringing an end to something.

MAGICAL PROPERTIES OF COFFEE ROASTS

As mentioned in the first chapter, coffee beans are roasted to get their flavor—roasting levels provide a different flavor and caffeine level. For everyday coffee, you need to only worry about three roasts: light, medium, and dark. You can use whatever coffee roast flavor you prefer in your craft; there are certain magical properties that are associated with each roast:

LIGHT ROAST

For light roast coffee, the beans have been roasted for the least amount of time, allowing them to keep their original flavor. The higher the quality of coffee, the lighter the roast. This roast makes a thinner, milder cup of coffee with a fruity note. While the flavor is more delicate than the other two roasts, it is more acidic and has more caffeine. Light roast is best prepared using a pour-over method to brew.

Types of Light Roast: Cinnamon, half-city, New England, light city, and white coffee.

Magical Properties: Energy, clarity, patience, motivation, friendship, honesty, impartiality, abundance, healing.

MEDIUM ROAST

Medium roast is the most common coffee roast as it seems to be everyone's favorite. This is partly because it's so versatile—you can add just about anything to a medium roast. These coffee beans roast longer than lighter roast coffee, bringing out more flavor the longer it roasts. Medium roast coffee is less acidic, bringing more balance to the brew. This roast has a nutty, chocolaty taste that is favored by many taste buds. A medium roast can brew in many ways: drip brew, French press, cold brew, air over, moka pot, and can even be made into an espresso. The possibilities are endless.

Types of Medium Roast: Full city, breakfast blend, regular roast, American.

Magical Properties: Balance, flexibility, adaption, prosperity, strength, creativity, reliability, grounding, and determination.

DARK ROAST

Last, we have the dark side of coffee: the dark roast. On the polar end from light roast, dark roast coffee is roasted until the sugars in the beans start to caramelize and the oils begin to rise from out of the beans. Some even refer to this as "burnt" coffee because of how long the beans have to roast and because lower quality beans are usually used to make a dark roast. However, dark roast coffee has a strong smoky flavor that some may describe as bitter. While it has less caffeine than the other two roasts, it's often used in making lattes, cappuccinos, and mochaccinos, as the milk tends to soften the strong flavor. Dark roast coffee is best brewed in an espresso machine or a moka pot, as brewing for an extended period can make the coffee taste bitter.

Types of Dark Roast: French, Viennese, Italian, high roast, European, Spanish, Orleans, and Neapolitan.

Magical Properties: Deep meditation, divination, accuracy, introspection, precision, forethought, and foresight.

A SPLASH OF MILK AND MAGIC

While some of us savor black coffee, others need to add a little something extra to their brew for their personal preference. That is the beauty of coffee and why it works so well in witchcraft. It is a blank slate to which you can add whatever you like to get the taste you want and the magical benefits you desire. Whether you prefer to add milk, sugar, or a diary alternative to your cup, we have the magical associate for each, for when you need a little boost of luck, love, or balance.

- **Dairy Milk/Cream:** Dairy milk and cream of all kinds are associated with nurturing, protection, fortune, and some good vibes.
- **Soy Milk:** Provides protection, offers psychic powers, and boosts spirituality.
- **Oat Milk:** Provides grounding energy, increases determination, and increases focus.
- **Cashew Milk:** Provides strength and increases wealth.
- **Almond Milk:** Stirring in almond milk can provide wisdom, luck, and prosperity.
- **Coconut Milk:** Increases confidence, psychic awareness, spirituality, and protection.

MAGICAL HERBS AND SPICES

While we love a simple cup of coffee in the morning, a modern witch knows the magic of trying a new flavored coffee from their favorite brand or when their coffee shop has a new seasonal drink. These different flavors not only enchant our taste buds but also bring a little metaphysical boost to our lives. Why does adding a dash of cinnamon on top of our latte make us more creative? Why does adding chocolate syrup to our brew put us in a loving mood? We'll go over coffee recipes in Chapter Two, but here is an introduction to twenty-five common herbs and spices that are added to coffee. This is not a definitive list by any means, but it's a quick introduction to the different ingredients you can add to your coffee at home, especially if you wish to spice things up.

ALLSPICE

A common misconception is that allspice is made up of every spice combined into one. However, allspice is actually a spice on its own, made from dried pimento. The misunderstanding most likely comes from the name and the fact that it tastes like a blend of nutmeg, cloves, and cinnamon. A pinch of this can add a magical boost to your coffee.

Flavor Profile: Sweet and a little spicy.

Magical Properties: Money, luck, healing, treasure, determination, and energy.

Health Properties: Helps reduce inflammation, ease headaches, alleviate muscle pain, and reduce bloating and gas.

Ways to Add to Coffee: Add a pinch of ground allspice to your cup of coffee; sprinkle into coffee grounds.

Medical Warning: Large quantities may cause nausea and vomiting.

APPLE

An apple a day is supposed to keep the doctor away, but it may bring a coven of witches to your door. Apples have always had a bewitching energy around them—and not just because of their association with autumn. In mythology, apple trees were considered one of the most sacred trees, representing good health and happiness. Apples are associated with Aphrodite, the goddess of love. And let's not forget about Eve and the apple…

Flavor Profile: A little sweet and a little tart.

Magical Properties: Love, knowledge, immortality, temptation, divination, health, gratitude, generosity, creativity, fertility, and abundance.

Health Properties: Rich in antioxidants, fiber, and vitamin C. Anti-inflammatory, promotes gut health, protects heart, boosts brain health.

Ways to Add to Coffee: Combine dried apples with ground coffee and brew; apple cider, apple syrup, apple-flavored creamers.

Medical Warning: None.

BLUEBERRY

A sign of summertime, blueberries are becoming a very popular coffee flavor during the spring and summer months when we can all use a sweet pick-me-up in the morning. Blueberries are native to North America and were frequently used in the medical practice of different Indigenous tribes.

Flavor Profile: Ranging from sweet to tart, depending on ripeness.

Magical Properties: Youthfulness, optimism, beauty, calmness, protection; enhances memory and increases intuition.

Health Properties: Rich in antioxidants, anti-inflammatory, relieves stomach problems, can help lower blood pressure, improves vision, boosts heart health, improves memory, and boosts mood.

Ways to Add to Coffee: Blueberry syrup, blueberry-flavored ground coffee, blueberry coffee creamer, muddled blueberries.

Medical Warning: Diabetics should be cautious when consuming an excess amount of blueberries as they can make blood sugar too low.

CARAMEL

Coffee and caramel are an iconic duo that go hand in hand with each other. A standard topper in iced lattes, fraps, and really any trendy coffee concoction. Caramel adds a lovely, sweet taste to cut the sometimes-acidic tones of coffee for a sweet treat. For a bit of positivity to your coffee spells, add a little caramel.

Flavor Profile: Rich and sweet.

Magical Properties: Positivity, comfort, memory, self-love, friendship, transformation, tenacity. Caramel is also known to soothe our moods.

Health Properties: While we wouldn't consider caramel a "healthy food," it is good for the skin and has a surprising amount of antioxidants.

Ways to Add to Coffee: Caramel syrup or sauce, caramel extract added to ground coffee, caramel-flavored creamers.

Medical Warning: Too much caramel is not good for your body, teeth, and blood sugar. Moderation is key.

CARDAMOM

Cardamom is very popular in the Middle East, especially in a Turkish coffee drink with a sweet and floral taste. Add cardamom for a boost in intuition when doing a coffee divination reading. Cardamom was native to India before being introduced to Western culture by Alexander the Great. Since then, it's been used to spice up a variety of drinks and dishes.

Flavor Profile: Sets with a hint of lemon and mint. Black cardamom pods have a bit of smokiness.

Magical Properties: Clarity, courage, direction, wisdom, love, and lust.

Health Properties: Lowers blood pressure, is rich in antioxidants, relieves nausea, prevents cavities, treats infections, reduces bad breath, lowers blood sugar, reduces anxiety, protects the liver, and improves lung health.

Ways to Add to Coffee: Grind coffee beans and cardamom seeds together, then brew; put whole cardamom pods into Turkish coffee; cardamom syrup.

Medical Warning: None.

CAYENNE

If you're looking for a little kick to your morning coffee, add a sprinkle of cayenne to get things started. While cayenne might not be the first ingredient you reach for when you're brewing your coffee, it does add a little heat to bring out the rich smokiness in the coffee. Witches have loved cayenne for years, often using it for revenge. It was believed that sprinkling cayenne around an enemy's house would make them leave that person alone.

Flavor Profile: Slightly sweet with subtle smokiness and pepperiness.

Magical Properties: Cleansing, protection, strength, motivation, courage, removes obstacles, speeds things up (including spells, energy, and manifestations), opens roads, breaks hexes.

Health Properties: Heals heartburn, soothes a sore throat, relieves cold symptoms, boosts metabolism, reduces hunger, improves digestion, lowers blood pressure, and improves vision.

Ways to Add to Coffee: Sprinkle a little cayenne pepper powder directly into your coffee, blend cayenne powder with milk and sugar, and add cayenne pepper to ground coffee.

Medical Warning: This can cause stomach distress when eating too much of it; possible blood clotting.

CINNAMON

A seasonal flavor that can be used any time of the year to add a magical boost to your morning. While cinnamon is an ingredient in many popular holiday drinks (looking at you, pumpkin spice), it also tastes great on its own.

Flavor Profile: Sweet, woody, with a spicy edge.

Magical Properties: Luck, success, energy, happiness, creativity, wealth, psychic boost, healing, protection, love magic, communication with the spirit world, sun magic, and fire energy.

Health Properties: Reduces blood sugar, helps heal chronic wounds, boosts heart health, helps with digestion, improves memory, and lowers blood pressure.

Ways to Add to Coffee: Sprinkle a pinch of cinnamon directly in your coffee or on top of lattes, add cinnamon to your ground coffee, swirl a cinnamon stick in your coffee; cinnamon-flavored creamers, and cinnamon syrup.

Medical Warning: Limit cinnamon to one teaspoon a day. Ask your doctor about your cinnamon intake if you're being treated for diabetes.

CHOCOLATE

Like coffee, chocolate has a very magical history. Originating in Mesoamerica, chocolate was made from roasted and ground cacao seeds. Mexican people believed that cocoa was a gift from Quetzalcoatl, the god of wisdom. Chocolate was often used in rituals, ceremonies, spells, and sometimes as a form of currency. We can see the magic today when a bite of chocolate is all it takes to improve our mood.

Flavor Profile: Milk chocolate has a mild, velvety-sweet taste, while dark chocolate is more bitter.

Magical Properties: Prosperity, self-love, friendship, replenishing magical energy, nurturing, love, grounding, balance, increased emotional energy, ancestral magic, lust.

Health Properties: Rich in antioxidants, can increase neurological happiness, improves memories, decreases depression symptoms, boosts longevity, reduces the risk of stroke, and strengthens the immune system.

Ways to Add to Coffee: Cocoa powder, chocolate syrup, cocoa nibs, and chopped up.

Medical Warning: Chocolate does have caffeine, so keep it in moderation (especially mixed with coffee) if you have a caffeine sensitivity. Keep this away from your four-legged familiars.

CLOVES

A wintertime favorite, cloves can quickly warm you up on a bitterly cold morning and warm your heart up with its cozy scene. Cloves are commonly used in Chinese traditional medicine and Ayurvedic medicines. Kitchen witches love the spice for their seasonal baking and the magic it can provide.

Flavor Profile: Warm and slightly sweet.

Magical Properties: Protection, love, abundance, banishing negativity, courage, prosperity, warmth.

Health Properties: Full of antioxidants, promotes a healthy liver, eases toothaches, helps treat sinus infections, aids in digestion, reduces fever.

Ways to Add to Coffee: Add cloves to ground coffee before brewing.

Medical Warning: Ask your doctor before taking cloves if you have a bleeding or blood-clotting disorder or are about to have surgery.

GINGER

Native to Southeast Asia, ginger is one of the world's oldest recognized medicinal plants, first being mentioned in Chinese writing in 400 BC. It is a superfood that is one of the world's biggest sources of antioxidants. For everything from treating medical ailments to spicing up your favorite treats, ginger can really give you an emotional and spiritual boost. A popular beverage in Yemen is called "qishr," a hot drink mixed with extra-fine ground coffee, ginger powder, water, and sugar.

Flavor Profile: Sweet and slightly peppery.

Magical Properties: Confidence, clarity, sensuality, quick manifestation, energy boost, inner power, healing, abundance, passion, balance, success, and retribution.

Health Properties: Anti-inflammatory, helps end nausea, eases arthritis pain, can help lower cholesterol, and reduces colds.

Ways to Add to Coffee: Add ground ginger to coffee or mix in with coffee grounds, add crystallized ginger to coffee, or add freshly grated ginger root to coffee grounds; ginger syrup, and gingerbread flavor creamers.

Medical Warning: Talk to your doctor about taking excess ginger if you have a heart condition, diabetes, and/or have gallstones.

HAZELNUT

One of the most popular flavors to add to your favorite cup of coffee or latte, hazelnut imparts a little creamy sweetness to your cup. Hazelnuts are also pretty magical within themselves, as the branches from the hazel tree have often been used in making wands. Use a little hazelnut to cast a spell on your brew.

Flavor Profile: Nutty, creamy, and a little earthy.

Magical Properties: Creativity, inspiration, luck, fertility, self-love, compassion, enhances witchcraft.

Health Properties: Regulates blood pressure, reduces inflammation, supports heart health.

Ways to Add to Coffee: Hazelnut extract, hazelnut syrup, hazelnut creamer; grind hazelnut and coffee beans together.

Medical Warning: Do not take it if you have a severe nut allergy.

HONEY

Coffee is famous for keeping us buzzing and busy, so it's only natural to think that adding some honey to our coffee will really take the sting out of getting up in the morning. Honey has been a valued part of many ancient civilizations, including ancient Egypt, where honey was used in the mummification process. Honey is also a great substitute for sugar, as it makes our coffee sweet without the high sugar content.

Flavor Profile: Generally sweet but can have floral, smoky, fruity, or earthy notes depending on the type of honey.

Magical Properties: Sweetens situations, replenishes magical energy, binds, heals, cleanses, provides love; kindness, wealth, community, positivity, happiness, deity offering, fairy magic, passion, and spirituality.

Health Properties: Reduces anxiety, rich in antioxidants, improves heart health, heals wounds, soothes the throat, suppresses coughs, strengthens the immune system, improves the skin, and eases sinus issues.

Ways to Add to Coffee: Fresh or jar honey, honeycombs.

Medical Warning: Not safe for babies under one year old.

LAVENDER

Quickly becoming one of the most popular latte flavors because of its "bougie" vibes and aesthetic. Witches have loved lavender for thousands of years, using the magical flavor to protect their homes and bring peace to their lives. Native to the Mediterranean, India, and the Middle East, but you can grow lavender almost anywhere.

Flavor Profile: Sweet and earthy.

Magical Properties: Happiness, healing, love, protection, prosperity, relaxation, sleep aid dream magic, peace of mind.

Health Properties: Decreases anxiety, decreases insomnia, helps with depression symptoms, eases headaches, decreases nausea, and helps with pain. Eases acne issues and skin irritation.

Ways to Add to Coffee: Lavender syrup; add dried lavender petals to ground coffee or on top of lattes for garnish.

Medical Warning: Do not take with a sedative.

LEMON

Seeing lemon on this list may be quite the head-scratcher: coffee and lemon? It seems like they are complete opposite of each other. However, while we wouldn't suggest putting lemon juice in light roast coffee or mochas, adding a twist of lemon to an espresso or dark roast coffee can cut the coffee's bitterness.

Flavor Profile: Tangy and sour.

Magical Properties: Purification, happiness, beauty, longevity, love, openness, clarity, friendship, sun magic; removes hexes.

Health Properties: Lowers the risk of heart disease, lowers cholesterol, helps absorb iron, improves digestion, lowers blood pressure, boosts the immune system, eases cold symptoms, and soothes sore throats.

Ways to Add in Coffee: Add lemon rind to espresso; lemon juice and lemonade.

Medical Warning: Drinking too much lemon juice can damage the enamel on your teeth, can worsen gastroesophageal reflux disease, and worsen heartburn.

MAPLE

Next to the classic pumpkin spice latte, maple lattes are an autumnal staple in coffee shops all over. Associated with the witchy season, maple trees are connected with change—their leaves turning from one color to another until they eventually fall off and move on. Maple reminds us to adapt and move slowly through life.

Flavor Profile: Sweet, with hints of caramel and vanilla.

Magical Properties: Love, money, longevity, travel, learning, decision-making, dealing with change, spiritual healing, protection, abundance, and adaptability.

Health Properties: While I wouldn't suggest having maple syrup for every meal like Buddy the Elf, pure maple syrup, in moderation, can have some surprising health benefits, including being a healthier alternative to sugar, boosting brain health, and lowering cholesterol.

Ways to Add to Coffee: Maple syrup, maple extract, maple-flavor creamer.

Medical Warning: Too much maple syrup (especially fake, sugary maple syrup) can lead to tooth decay when consumed in excess and can raise blood sugar and insulin levels.

MOLASSES

A smoky-sweet alternative to maple syrup, molasses can add extra depth to your coffee, especially during the holiday season when gingerbread coffee dominates. Magically, molasses and coffee seem like a contradiction, with speedy, energetic coffee meeting slow-moving molasses, but together, they help you slow down and realize what's truly important, like a second cup of coffee.

Flavor Profile: Warm, sweet, and a little smoky.

Magical Properties: Slowing situations, sweetening feelings, overcoming enemies, sticking to situations, increasing drive; money, wisdom, business success, binding spells.

Health Properties: While probably not the healthiest thing you can put in your coffee every morning, molasses is a better source of antioxidants than sugar, helps maintain strong bones, and can control blood sugar.

Ways to Add to Coffee: Pour a little molasses into your coffee; molasses-flavored creamer.

Medical Warning: Use in moderation, as even molasses still has sugar than may not be good for you over time.

NUTMEG

This is another holiday favorite that is good for any time of the year when you just want a little extra spice in your cup of coffee.

Witches love to add it to coffee when going on a big trip as nutmeg is the ultimate travel partner—both on the physical and spiritual plane.

Flavor Profile: Sweet and nutty.

Magical Properties: Luck, travel, lucid dreaming, attraction, psychic visions, getting legal justice, prosperity, lust.

Health Properties: Eases arthritis pain, increases sex drive, prevents gum diseases, boosts mood, improves memory and heart health.

Ways to Add to Coffee: Sprinkle nutmeg powder or grated nutmeg in brewed coffee or in ground coffee before brewing.

Medical Warning: Too much nutmeg can cause hallucinations and loss of coordination.

PEPPERMINT

You know it's winter when peppermint mochas are back on the menu in your local coffee shop. However, peppermint doesn't just bring out holiday magic. It is also wonderful for finding your voice (especially if you have a sore throat) and bringing a little luck and wealth into your life. So, drink up!

Flavor Profile: Minty.

Magical Properties: Positive thoughts, luck, inspiration, divination, prosperity, cleansing, healing, mental clarity, speaking up, and protection.

Health Properties: Eases tension headaches, reduces nasal congestion, helps decrease bloating and gas, eases nausea, reduces seasonal allergies, helps with an upper respiratory infection, soothes a sore throat, and provides a boost of energy.

Ways to Add to Coffee: Peppermint syrup, peppermint extract, peppermint-flavored creamers; grind coffee beans and fresh mint together.

Medical Warning: None.

RASPBERRY

If you're looking to add a little sweetness and a little tartness to your coffee, consider adding a taste of raspberry to your brew. An increasingly popular coffee flavor pairing during Valentine's Day (especially paired with chocolate), this ingredient is really feeling the love, as it was once considered the prized fruit of Greek gods. According to Greek mythology, Ida the nymph used raspberry to heal Zeus's sorrows.

Flavor Profile: Sweet, tart.

Magical Properties: Faith, jubilation, commitment, confidence, attraction, protection, healing, love, strength, endurance, fertility, kindness, compassion, desire, creativity, sweetness, sex magic, and reliability.

Health Properties: Can alleviate arthritis pain, improves balance, protects skin from sun damage, and combats signs of aging.

Ways to Add to Coffee: Raspberry syrup, raspberry extract.

Medical Warning: None.

ROSE

While not considered a traditional coffee additive, rose is quickly becoming popular in everything from pour-overs to lattes. Roses are often associated with Aphrodite, the Greek goddess of love and beauty, making us all feel extra romantic.

Flavor Profile: Sweet and fruity.

Magical Properties: Love in all its forms, glamour, divination, healing, psychic abilities, compassion, protection, and calm.

Health Properties: Anti-inflammatory; reduces anxiety, increases heart health, relieves stress, improves the skin, and gives a mental boost for clarity.

Ways to Add to Coffee: Rose water, rose simple syrup, culinary roses.

Medical Warning: Not recommended if you have a rose allergy or are on blood thinners or antidepressants.

ROSEMARY

While most commonly found in your spice cabinet for savory dishes, rosemary can also be added to your coffee for a unique blend of flavor. While it may not be the most common coffee pairing, it is a great study tool if you're up late working on a paper or cramming for a test, as rosemary is associated with memory, concentration, and intellect. So, drink up!

Flavor Profile: Citrus and pine with a bit of mint.

Magical Properties: Love, luck, intuition, cleansing, strength, protection, invigoration, virtue, memory, fidelity.

Health Properties: Improves memory and concentration, boosts mood, reduces anxiety, protects vision, promotes digestion and hair growth, and lowers blood sugar.

Ways to Add to Coffee: Add a fresh sprig to ground coffee before brewing; rosemary syrup.

Medical Warning: Do not consume large quantities when on an anticoagulant, ACE inhibitors, diuretics, or lithium.

STAR ANISE

Star anise is one of the most magical-looking spices out there because it is literally in the shape of a star. Tied to a string, it can act as a pendulum when you want to do a divination reading while sipping your coffee.

Flavor Profile: Licorice.

Magical Properties: Psychic powers, luck, happiness, protection, dreams, youth, falling in love, divination, spiritual aid.

Health Properties: Relieves gas, bloating, and cramps; calms nervousness; brings sleep; and relieves cough, bronchitis, and asthma.

Ways to Add in Coffee: Add roasted or raw star anise to coffee and brew, add to whole beans and grind them together.

Medical Warning: While star anise is safe for adults, it looks similar to Japanese star anise, which is poisonous. Remember to buy star anise from a reputable supplier to avoid confusion.

SUGAR

Sugar, spice, and everything nice makes for a perfect cup of coffee. Perfect for sweetening your day or your feelings, sugar has long been used in love magic and is a way to multiply and amplify your magic. Take a spoonful of sugar in your coffee and stir clockwise to activate any spell or intention you wish to bring to life.

Flavor Profile: Sweet.

Magical Properties: Attraction, love, glamour, prosperity, smoothing things over, manifesting, multiplying.

Health Properties: While we wouldn't call sugar the "healthiest" ingredient on this list, it does provide short-term energy, boost mood, and exfoliate the skin.

Ways to Add to Coffee: Put some sugar or sugar substitute directly in your coffee.

Medical Warnings: Sugar should only be used in small doses as too much can harm your body's health and the health of your teeth.

TURMERIC

For a golden morning, you need to add a golden spice to your life to give it an extra boost. Turmeric is a popular spice because its roots contain a yellow chemical called curcumin, which is not only very healing, but also turns into a lovely orange color when ground up. Perfect for changing the color of your coffee and making things a little more golden.

Flavor Profile: Warm but bitter.

Magical Properties: Protection, health, fertility, banishment, vitality, blessings, and golden opportunities.

Health Properties: Can boost brain development, improves memory, relieves heartburn, lowers the risk of heart disease, eases arthritis pain, lessens symptoms of depression, promotes longevity, is an anti-inflammatory, is a powerful antioxidant, and can reduce the symptoms of hay fever.

Ways to Add to Coffee: Turmeric powder, turmeric extract.

Medical Warning: Do not take it if you have gallbladder issues; bleeding disorders; endometriosis; breast, uterine, or ovarian cancer; uterine fibroids, or an iron deficiency. Do not consume two weeks before surgery.

VANILLA

Vanilla is often synonymous with "boring" or "plain," but that couldn't be further from the truth. While the flavor may be sweet and delicate, vanilla is a hard plant to obtain, with its limited pollination season and difficult growing season. Next to saffron, vanilla is the most expensive spice to buy. So be a little kinder when talking about vanilla.

Flavor Profile: Sweet, creamy, floral.

Magical Properties: Inner peace, love, happiness, luck, lust, passion, friendship, calm, strength, healing, positivity, comfort, vitality, mental quickness, and beauty.

Health Properties: An anti-inflammatory; fights acne; increases hair growth; reduces intestinal distress, fever, and anxiety; prevents tooth decay.

Ways to Add to Coffee: Vanilla extract, vanilla syrup, vanilla-flavor creamer, vanilla bean.

Medical Warning: Vanilla can cause headaches and insomnia.

COMMON COFFEE DRINKS AND THEIR MAGICAL MEANINGS

In Chapter Two, we'll go over different coffee recipes for every magical situation. But let's first look at the most common kinds of coffee drinks to truly understand what we're brewing. A red eye is very different from a cappuccino, and, therefore, will have different magical properties that can make or break a spell. Let's see what makes the most popular coffee drinks percolate.

ESPRESSO

There's always been some confusion around espresso: Is it coffee? Is it different from coffee? Does it come from the same plant? The answer is that espresso is indeed coffee and comes from the same coffee beans. However, espresso is a stronger, thicker version of coffee with a much higher caffeine level. Espresso is made by forcing nearly boiling water through very finely ground coffee, creating a more potent brew than regular coffee. Because of its taste and caffeine content, it's usually served in smaller quantities and referred to as a "shot." While you couldn't (or shouldn't) drink a steaming mug full of espresso, it's great for quick spells and rituals and is usually the base in many drink recipes. You can also eat chocolate-covered espresso beans if you're doing a spell on the go.

Magical Properties: Energy, clarity, protection, banishment, awareness, creativity, speed, productivity, casting and breaking curses.

RED EYE

For most people, coffee is one of the few things that can keep their eyes open in the morning. However, if you've had a long night, a simple cup of coffee isn't going to cut it. That's where the red eye comes in. Originally known as "a shot in the dark," a red eye is coffee with an espresso shot poured on top. Unlike most coffees on this list that have a long history, the red eye is a '90s baby, starting life as a secret Starbucks menu hack that quickly spread through word of mouth. Its name comes from the red-eye flights that travel from coast to coast in the middle of the night. You'll need a strong cup of coffee after one of those.

Magical Properties: Divination, glamour, curses, clarity, increasing intensity of a spell or intention.

AMERICANO

For when you want a cup of coffee but only have an espresso shot, try an Americano! An Americano is simply a shot or two of espresso with hot water poured in, giving it the same volume and strength as regular coffee while keeping the flavor of espresso. The popular myth about the drink is that it got its name during the Second World War when American soldiers stationed in Italy poured water into espresso to make it look like the coffee they had back in the States. However, the term has appeared in writing as early as the late 1920s. It's still good for those who want to sip espresso for longer.

Magical Properties: Productivity, quickness, independence, adaptability, multiplying, strength, energy.

CAFÉ AU LAIT

While it has a fancy name, café au lait is French for "coffee with milk." This simple but tasty drink is just coffee with steamed milk on top. This is slightly different from regular coffee with cream (also known as a "white coffee"), as you must use hot milk instead of cold milk or creamers. In Spain, this drink is known as *café con leche*. It is a popular drink in New Orleans, where it is made with scalded milk and mixed with chicory. Paired with a beignet, it makes for a tasty snack.

Magical Properties: Comfort, sleep, peace, blessings, positivity.

LATTE

A coffee shop standard, the caffè latte, also known as a just a latte, is one of the most popular coffee-based drinks. A latte has an espresso base with steamed milk and some foamed milk on top. However, one would use espresso and chilled milk poured over ice when making an iced latte. Lattes are popular because you can add any flavor combination to them, from chai latte (with or without tea) to the super-popular pumpkin spice latte, and everything in between.

Magical Properties: Luck, blessings, creativity, pleasantries, and fertility.

CAPPUCCINO

A coffeehouse favorite, cappuccino is an espresso-based coffee drink from Italy. Cappuccino gets its name from the Capuchin friars, as the colors of their habits match the color of the drink. A cappuccino has espresso at its base, followed by steamed milk with thick foam on top. Cappuccinos and lattes differ because cappuccinos have distinct layers of espresso, steamed milk, and milk foam, while a latte has the espresso and the steamed milk mixed together. Cappuccinos also have an even amount of espresso, steamed milk, and milk foam, while a latte only has a little milk foam on top.

Magical Properties: Strength, focus, prosperity, communication, divination, peace, balance.

FLAT WHITE

Another edition of "Is this a latte?" we have the flat white, which is commonly mistaken for the latte. However, it is actually more of a fancy, sophisticated version of a latte as it is made with espresso and microfoam, a steamed milk with small bubbles and a velvet consistency. While you can add flavors to a latte, a flat white allows the espresso to be the star flavor while the microfoam adds texture. The foam also creates sip rings with each sip for a visual feature.

Magical Properties: Glamour, abundance, patience, memorability, divination.

MACCHIATO

The last installment of our "espresso and milk foam" series, we have the macchiato, also known as the espresso macchiato. This is an espresso drink with a small amount of milk foam in the center. In Italian, macchiato means "stained" or "spotted," so caffè macchiato translates into "stained coffee." This coffee started life as a teaching tool as it comes from baristas showing waiters the difference between a plain espresso and one with a small amount of milk. However, thanks to big coffee chains, the definition of the drink has changed to being a beverage with a lot of milk, an espresso shot, and plenty of syrup and caramel. The traditional macchiato is ideal for people who want to try espresso but may need a little milk to ease the taste.

Magical Properties: Growth, travel, protection, catalyst for change, movement, and divination.

MOCHA

A more grown-up version of the cozy hot chocolate we loved as kids, a caffè mocha, or "mocha" for short, is a coffee drink made with chocolate, espresso, and steamed milk with whipped cream on top. The drink originated in Italy but was named after the city of Mocha in Yemen, which was one of the centers of the early coffee trade. Unlike most coffee drinks, mocha is traditionally served in a glass rather than a mug.

Magical Properties: Love, friendship, forgiveness, emotions, and luck.

ICED COFFEE

Basic witches can't seem to get enough iced coffee. An iced coffee is exactly what it says in the name: a coffee served on ice. While this iced version of our favorite brew has grown popular in recent years as a staple for any season, it's been around for longer than we think. The first iced coffee, called a "Mazagran," originated in Algeria in 1840. A Mazagran is made with coffee syrup and cold water. The first time iced coffee was marketed to the public was in the 1920s, but it really took off in the 2010s when big fast-food chains started to offer the drink in various flavors. You can get any version of coffee, especially lattes, iced. Perfect for those who hate when their hot coffee gets cold.

Magical Properties: Motivation, courage, success, wealth, confidence; works best for career spells.

COLD BREW

A coffee novice may get iced coffee and cold brew confused as they sound very similar—they're both cold right? However, a cold brew isn't just a coffee on ice but a specific method of brewing coffee. Cold brew is similar to drip coffee, but instead of coffee grounds being steeped in boiling water, it's steeped in cold water through a coffee filter or a French press. It also takes longer than drip coffee, as cold brew needs around eight to twenty-four hours to steep. This produces a stronger coffee flavor with much more caffeine. Cold brew originated in Japan; it is their traditional way to brew coffee. While cold brew is usually served on ice, you can heat it up after it's finished steeping.

Magical Properties: Divination, intuition, balance, justice, level-headedness, slowing things down, strength.

FRAPPÉ

If you're a fan of big coffee chains and have a bit of a sweet tooth, you're probably all too familiar with frappés, a Greek iced coffee traditionally made with instant coffee, water, sugar, and milk. Modern frappés are made with espresso, milk, flavored syrup, and whipped cream. While it's the most popular coffee in Greece, the name is actually French, meaning a drink chilled with ice. Frappés were created in 1957 in Thessaloniki, Greece, when a Nescafé representative, Dimitris Vakondios, was showing a new product aimed at children: a chocolate drink made instantly with a shaker. On a coffee break, Vakondios put some instant coffee in the shaker. The drink instantly took off and the rest is history.

Magical Properties: Tranquility, love, connection, sweetness, youth, pleasure.

AFFOGATO

Coffee and ice cream are a common dessert served after a good meal. However, why not save time and combine the two? That is the beauty of the affogato. Traditionally known as an affogato al caffè (drowned in coffee), this is a coffee-based dessert where you take a cup of espresso and put a scoop of ice cream or gelato in it. Those who wish for a booze kick can add amaretto, Kahlúa, or other liquor to the drink for a wicked finish.

Magical Properties: Joy, fulfillment, happiness, creativity, luck, lust, satisfaction.

Chapter 2

BEWITCHED BREWS

Coffee is magical on its own, but combining it with other spices and ingredients can truly make it spellbinding. Anyone who's ever set foot in a cafe knows there are an almost endless amount of ways to add to a cup of coffee, with everything from maple lattes to peppermint mochas. And when you combine the right ingredients with an intent, you can make something magical. Even if you just need to get through the day. You are the alchemist, creating the right caffeinated mix to make your dreams come true.

BASIC WITCHES' BREW
A magical power-up potion

Naturally, I had to start a book about coffee witchcraft with *the* witchiest coffee there is: the pumpkin spice latte. This bewitching brew enchants coffee lovers every autumn. What is it about the PSL that's got everyone under its spell? It's a potion that has a little bit of everything a modern witch needs in this world: luck, protection, abundance, energy, success, happiness, creativity, and even some love. If you feel you need a magical boost of *something*, but you're not sure what, conjure up this witches' brew that's anything but basic.

———— ·❈· ————

1 cup coconut milk (*psychic awareness, spirituality, and protection*)

¼ cup water

2 tablespoons pumpkin purée (*gratitude, generosity, abundance, potential, protection, and stability*)

½ teaspoon ground cinnamon (*luck, success, energy, happiness, creativity, money, psychic boost, healing, love magic*)

¼ teaspoon ground ginger (*confidence, clarity, quick manifestation, energy boost, inner power, healing, abundance, passion, balance, success*)

⅛ teaspoon ground nutmeg (*luck, travel, attraction, prosperity*)

⅛ teaspoon ground allspice (*money, luck, healing, determination, and energy*)

⅛ teaspoon ground cardamom (*clarity, courage, direction, wisdom, love*)

⅛ teaspoon ground black pepper *(cleansing, protection, shield for jealousy, motivation, focus)*

1 ounce brewed espresso *(energy, clarity, protection, banishment, awareness, creativity, productivity)*

½ teaspoon vanilla extract *(inner peace, love, happiness, luck, passion, friendship, calm, strength, healing, positivity, comfort, vitality, mental quickness, and beauty)*

2 teaspoons maple syrup *(love, money, longevity, travel, learning, decision-making, dealing with change, spiritual healing, protection, abundance, and adaptability)*

HOW TO BREW

STEP 1: Heat up the coconut milk and water in a saucepan and bring to a simmer.

STEP 2: Add in the pumpkin purée, the spices, the black pepper, and maple syrup. Whisk until smooth, stirring clockwise.

STEP 3: Add in the espresso, vanilla extract, and maple syrup. Whisk until smooth.

STEP 4: Pour into your cup and enjoy. You can also add a dollop of whipped cream (coconut or regular) and a little cinnamon or pumpkin spice on top for garnish. Enjoy!

MAGIC TRICKS

If you don't have a stovetop or just don't feel like using one, combine the milk and water together in a microwave-safe bowl. Add the pumpkin purée, spices, black pepper, maple, and vanilla. Microwave for a minute and a half. Whisk until foamy. Add into your mug of espresso.

If you don't have pumpkin purée or the spices on hand, add three tablespoons of pumpkin spice syrup to the bottom of your cup, add in your espresso, and stir. Then add some heated, frothed milk on top. Even easier, make some pumpkin spice coffee (either store-bought or brewed with coffee grounds and pumpkin spice mixed together) and add frothed milk on top.

FOR A DASH OF MAGIC...

Since this drink is meant to be a magical "booster," it's a great beverage to have after the "Cleanse Me in Coffee" ritual on page 116 to help raise your emotional and spiritual levels.

If you're trying to attract something specific into your life (money, love, success, etc.), write a sigil for that on the top of your latte to help attract it using "Draw Me a Spell" on page 147.

I LOVE ME A LATTE
A self-love potion

Let's face it, sometimes we aren't feeling our best selves. We become overly critical and unable to see the good within. Whether you need a pick-me-up or a confidence boost, this lovely latte is the perfect way to view yourself in an enchanting light. Even making it for yourself is an act of self-love.

---

1 cup vanilla soy milk *(happiness, love, protection, spirituality)*

8 cardamom pods, slightly crushed *(clarity, direction, courage, love)*

½ teaspoon rose water *(self-love, compassion, healing, calming, glamour)*

2 shots espresso or 2 tablespoons instant espresso *(clarity, awareness, energy)*

2 teaspoons dried rose petals *(self-love, compassion, healing, calmness, glamour)*

1 piece of rose quartz *(self-love)*

HOW TO BREW

STEP 1: Pour your vanilla soy milk into a saucepan. Add in your cardamom and rose water and stir on low heat until the milk is scalded.

STEP 2: Remove the cardamom pods from the brew and whisk the milk to froth it.

STEP 3: Take your favorite mug and pour in your espresso. If you're using instant espresso powder, make sure you mix it with a couple ounces of water.

STEP 4: Pour your rose milk froth on top of the espresso. Sprinkle the rose petals on top.

STEP 5: Take your rose quartz in your left hand and your drink in your right. Close your eyes and say three times: "I make myself this drink because I care about myself. Nurturing myself is an act of self-love. May this drink remind me that I love myself for all that I am."

STEP 6: Sip and enjoy.

MAGIC TRICKS

☀ If you want your latte to be a light pink color, add ½ teaspoon pink food coloring gel to the milk.

☀ If you don't have rose water on hand, adding rose syrup will work.

FOR A DASH OF MAGIC...

☀ Add some chocolate flakes or chocolate syrup to the top of your milk froth as chocolate is associated with self-love.

☀ For best results, make this brew on a Friday because that day is associated with the planet Venus, which is ideal for love spells.

☀ For best results, make this brew during a waning crescent moon since it is the phase associated with self-care and rest.

RED EYE FOR THE THIRD EYE
Wake up that sixth sense

Most people believe that only a gifted few can see into the future. However, that is not the case. Every single person has been born with intuition and a sixth sense to see into the future. That's because we are all born with a third eye (also known as the sixth chakra) that helps us see past the physical realm and into the spiritual realm and beyond. The difficulty is that not everyone has their third eye open. Fortunately, we can wake up our third eye with a tasty red eye coffee that can kick us into high gear and allow us to see the future with clarity and focus.

---

1 cup blueberry coffee (*increase in intuition, associated with the third-eye chakra*)

1 shot espresso or 1 tablespoon espresso power (*energy, clarity, awareness*)

a twist of lemon rind (*clarity, openness, purification*)

HOW TO BREW

STEP 1: Brew your cup of blueberry coffee. You can do this by simply using blueberry-flavored ground coffee, beans, or pods. If you don't have blueberry-flavored coffee, you can add blueberry syrup to your brewed coffee.

STEP 2: Make your espresso. You can also use a tablespoon of espresso powder if you don't have brewed espresso on hand.

STEP 3: Pour your espresso into your coffee.

STEP 4: Take your lemon rind and rub it around the rim of your coffee cup three times. As you do this, imagine that you clear out all the negative self-talk and doubt from your mind, leaving only clarity.

STEP 5: When you're finished, plop the rind into your drink and stir three times.

STEP 6: Take the coffee cup in your hand, close your physical eyes, and breathe in the aroma of the coffee. When you do this, imagine your third eye opening up.

STEP 7: Sip your coffee and meditate.

FOR A DASH OF MAGIC...

- Place a sigil for divination under your cup for a boost of intuition (see the "Sigil Magic" section on page 144 for more details).

- Use amethyst-infused water when making your coffee and/or espresso for a psychic boost.

- Use an indigo cup because it is associated with the third eye.

- For best results, make this drink on a Monday, as it is ruled by the moon, the best day for divination.

- Brew this drink to perform the "Are You Seer-ing This?" ritual on page 111 for an extra psychic boost.

- Sip this during your "Coffee and Cards" tarot reading on page 107 for a boost of intuition.

PEPPERMINT PERK UP

A brew to add a boost to all areas of your life

Coffee is famous for being able to wake you when you need a boost, be it in the morning when you first arise or at 3 p.m. when you're in a slump and need a break. However, what if *every* part of you is running on empty: emotionally, mentally, and spiritually? Fortunately, this tasty little drink will help you get your sparkle back.

½ cup espresso *(energy, clarity, awareness, speed, productivity). You can also use a cup of strong coffee.*

4 ounces heavy cream *(nurturing and some good vibe). You can also replace this with coconut milk for confidence and spirituality.*

2 tablespoons cocoa powder *(self-love, replenishing magical energy, nurturing, grounding, balance, increased emotional energy)*

½ teaspoon peppermint extract *(positive thoughts, inspiration, cleansing, healing, mental clarity, speaking up)*

¼ teaspoon vanilla extract *(inner peace, happiness, passion, calm, strength, healing, comfort, vitality, mental quickness, and beauty)*

HOW TO BREW

STEP 1: Brew your espresso or coffee. While that is brewing, heat up your heavy cream.

STEP 2: Pour your cocoa powder into your mug. Add in your espresso or coffee.

STEP 3: When your heavy cream is warm enough, pour it into your mug.

STEP 4: Add in your peppermint and vanilla extract. Stir all together three times, clockwise.

STEP 5: Sip and enjoy!

MAGIC TRICKS

⁕ If you have peppermint mocha–flavored coffee grounds or pods, brew that and add in the heavy cream.

⁕ This drink can be excellent cold as an iced coffee to bring motivation, courage, and confidence. Just don't heat the heavy cream and wait until the coffee is cooled before mixing.

⁕ You can make this into a true mocha by replacing heavy cream with steamed milk and adding whipped cream on top.

⁕ If you don't have peppermint extract, use peppermint syrup or crush a candy cane.

FOR A DASH OF MAGIC…

⁕ For a total perk up, sip this potion in the "Cleanse Me in Coffee" bath on page 116.

⁕ Drink this during your "Magic Morning Witch-ual" (page 96) for a bright start to your day.

⁕ For an extra boost, drink this after you perform the "Chakra Me Back to Life" ritual scrub on page 118.

⁕ For best results, brew this on a Tuesday. Tuesday is associated with Mars, the planet of energy, drive, and taking action.

LET'S STICK TOGETHER
A coffee for a closer relationship

Coffee is amazing at bringing people together, even during the most difficult times. In this modern world, it's hard to keep a coven together or even make a friendship last. This is a great potion to help you stay close to someone you care about with a sweet treat you can bond over. This is also an excellent brew to sip when celebrating a business or creative partnership or to help heal after a major falling out with friends.

ETHICAL NOTE: While this recipe for help bringing a relationship closer together, it isn't meant to forcibly bind someone to you or you to them. All humans have the power of free will. To try to take away someone's free will for your own personal gain can create a very sticky situation… and I'm not talking about the honey and molasses.

(Note this recipe makes enough for two people, but you can easily double the recipe to make more.)

½ cup of light roast ground coffee (*friendship, honesty, healing*)

1 cup cold water

1 cup milk (*any milk you prefer*)

1 tablespoon honey (*sweetening situations, replenishing magical energy, binding, love, kindness, community, positivity, offering*)

1 tablespoon molasses (*sweetening feelings, overcoming enemies, sticking to situations, wisdom, business success, binding*)

2 teaspoons granulated sugar *(attraction, love, manifesting, smoothing things over, multiplying)*

¼ teaspoon ground ginger *(clarity, healing, balance, success)*

¼ teaspoon ground cinnamon *(luck, success, energy, happiness, creativity, healing, protection, love magic)*

⅛ teaspoon ground nutmeg *(luck, attraction, prosperity)*

⅛ teaspoon ground cloves *(protection, love, abundance, banishing negativity, warmth)*

HOW TO BREW

STEP 1: Brew your coffee as usual using the coffee grounds and the cold water.

STEP 2: In a small pot, combine the milk, honey, molasses, sugar, and spices, and cook on medium heat.

STEP 3: Stir the mixture. As you stir, think about the person you are preparing this for and the relationship you hope to have with them. Channel all of these good vibes into your mixture.

STEP 4: When the mixture starts to steam, take it off the heat and pour it into a blender. Process for about 15 seconds until nice and foamy. As you blend, think about your energy and the other person's energy combining into one.

STEP 5: Take your coffee and pour it into two cups. Then, take your mixture and pour it into the cups.

STEP 6: Serve your coffee and click your glasses together. Enjoy.

FOR A DASH OF MAGIC...

☀ Write a friendship sigil in caramel sauce on the top of the drink. Caramel is associated with friendship, soothing, comfort, and transformation. See page 144 for "Sigil Magic"!

☀ For best results, make this on a Friday, as that is the day ruled by Venus and associated with relationships. Or on a Saturday, as Saturday is associated with Saturn, who rules over binding spells.

☀ This can also be done for someone who is not physically in the room with you. Just make the coffee and put their drink in front of a picture of them or a piece of paper with their name on it. This is a spiritual offering for that person.

☀ This is a great potion to serve at a coven meeting (or just a hangout with friends) to strengthen your bond and connection with each other. Simply double the recipe.

☀ If getting married, you and your partner may sip the brew before the wedding for a long-lasting union.

DEVIL'S BREW
A spellbinding brew to enchant your wild side

One of the nicknames for coffee is "Devil's Brew." To play with that idea, here's a sinfully delicious mocha that's perfect for helping you seduce your lover, practicing sex magic, or entering your villain era. Enjoy *wink*.

---

1 tablespoon hazelnut syrup (*enhancing witchcraft*)

1 cup brewed dark roast coffee (*divination, accuracy, introspection, precision, foresight*)

½ cup soy milk (*psychic powers, spirituality boost*)

1 tablespoon raspberry jam (*faith, sex magic, and desire*)

2 tablespoons cocoa powder (*replenishing magical energy, lust*)

whipped cream (*optional but fun *wink**)

fresh raspberries (*optional*)

HOW TO BREW

STEP 1: Pour your hazelnut syrup into a mug and stir. Add in your brewed coffee to the mug and stir.

STEP 2: In a microwave-safe bowl, add your milk, raspberry jam, and cocoa powder, and heat until combined (heat for 30-second intervals). Stir until creamy. If you don't have a microwave, heat and melt this on the stovetop.

STEP 3: Add the mixture to your coffee and stir. As you stir, think about the personal power and deep feelings you have within yourself.

STEP 4: Sip and enjoy. If you wish, you can add a little whipped cream and fresh raspberries for a fun touch…or use those for later. If sharing this with a lover, double the recipe. Just make sure they know what they're drinking.

MAGIC TRICKS

- You can swap out the hazelnut syrup for hazelnut coffee, either already flavored or made with ground and brewed unsalted hazelnuts.

- If you don't have hazelnut syrup, swap out the cocoa powder with two tablespoons of chocolate hazelnut spread.

FOR A DASH OF MAGIC...

- Make this during a full moon for an extra boost of magic.

- Use the "A Cup Full of Light" candle (page 132) when drinking to add a little fire and heat to your magic.

- Use your hazelnut syrup to write a sigil for magic, transformation, and sex on the bottom of your cup to infuse the magic (see page 147 for "Draw Me a Spell").

- Drink this wearing an outfit that makes you feel powerful (from a business suit to lingerie) to help boost your confidence.

- Drink this while holding or wearing carnelian to promote confidence, empowerment, and freedom.

- For best results, make this drink on a Tuesday, as it's associated with Mars, the planet of sex, power, and satisfying anger.

PIECE OF THE PIE
A potion to help you brew up money

Almost everyone has heard this budgeting "hack" at least once in their lives. "If you skip your daily coffee from the coffee shop, think of all the money you'll save!" While skipping your morning coffee run probably won't save you enough money to buy a house or get you out of crippling debt, this iced coffee potion may help bring a little more money and abundance into your life. Or at least save a little money by skipping the corporate coffee line.

---

1 cup medium roast coffee (*prosperity, reliability, determination*)

FOR THE APPLE SYRUP, MAKES ⅔ CUP
2 cups apple cider (*knowledge, gratitude, generosity, abundance*)

¼ cup maple syrup (*money, abundance*)

1 teaspoon cinnamon (*luck, success, money*)

½ teaspoon nutmeg (*luck, attraction, prosperity*)

½ teaspoon allspice (*money, luck, treasure*)

¼ teaspoon ground cloves (*abundance, banishing negativity, money*)

FOR THE ICED COFFEE
3 tablespoons of the apple syrup

½ cup cashew milk (*increase in wealth*)

1 cinnamon stick (*luck, success, money*)

ice cubes

HOW TO BREW

STEP 1: Start by making your coffee. Make it your preferred way and leave it out to cool. You can also use cold brew coffee if you prefer.

STEP 2: Prepare your apple syrup. In a saucepan, combine your apple cider and maple syrup. Add in your spices and stir.

STEP 3: Bring your mixture to a boil and simmer until it's reduced to one-third of its original volume. Take it off the heat and pour it into a bowl to cool and thicken up.

STEP 4: When cool, pour the apple syrup into a syrup bottle and refrigerate. This syrup should last up to a month.

STEP 5: Take your cold coffee and add in your syrup and milk and stir. Take your cinnamon stick and stir three times clockwise. As you stir, think about what you wish your financial situation were like—not just how much money you want or how stressed you feel about the lack of money, but how money can improve your life. Are you trying to get out of debt? Saving up to buy a house? Maybe you're seeking the safety and comfort that comes from having money in the bank? Act as though you already have it as you stir.

STEP 6: Drink and enjoy.

MAGIC TRICKS

- In a pinch, you can buy apple-flavored syrup or use apple-spiced coffee for this recipe.

- To make your iced coffee last longer, pour cold coffee (or apple cider and coffee in this brew) into ice cube containers. Freeze overnight. Take out some ice cubes and put them into your ice coffees or cold brews. As the ice melts, it'll add more coffee instead of water like regular ice cubes.

FOR A DASH OF MAGIC...

- You can also use the apple syrup in teas, pancakes, or other sweet treats. Pour a little over your snack for some of the money magic. Draw a sigil for money using the syrup for an added boost (see "Sigil Magic" on page 144).

- Swap out the maple syrup for molasses for business success.

- Swap out the maple syrup for granulated sugar to multiply your abundance, or add a pinch of sugar at the end to multiply your abundance.

- Use the "Just Like Magic" spell on page 154 to manifest your abundance as you stir.

- Hold a piece of pyrite or green aventurine as you drink for abundance and prosperity.

- For best results, brew this on a Thursday, which is ruled by Jupiter, associated with money spells.

- Drink this when casting the "Money Follows Wherever I Go" spell on page 186.

HOCUS POCUS, I REALLY NEED TO FOCUS

A magical cold brew latte to keep you focused

If you've ever had to pull an all-nighter or cram for a test, you know how important coffee is to keep you awake. However, you can only look at a screen, a textbook, or even work on a task for so long before you lose focus. When you find your mind wandering, take a small break to cook up this beautiful blue brew to help you get back on track.

---※---

10 ounces cold brew coffee *(intuition, balance, levelheadedness, slowing things down)*

½ cup vanilla oat milk *(grounding energy, determination, increase in focus, and mental quickness)*

¼ cup fresh or frozen blueberries *(optimism, memory enhancement, calming, protection, and increase in intuition)*

¼ teaspoon peppermint extract *(positive thoughts, luck, inspiration, mental clarity, speaking up)*

1 cardamom pod *(clarity, direction, wisdom)*

½ tablespoon maple syrup *(learning, decision-making, dealing with change, adaptability)*

ice cubes *(optional)*

---※---

HOW TO BREW

STEP 1: Make your cold brew. If you do not make your own cold brew, skip this step. You can also make this with regular iced coffee if you prefer.

STEP 2: Put your oat milk, blueberries, peppermint extract, cardamom, and maple syrup in a blender.

STEP 3: Blend until smooth and a lovely purple/blue color. Pour into a bowl or milk pitcher and use your milk frother, or a whisk, to froth your milk.

STEP 4: Take your cold brew and pour over ice, if using, in a tall glass. Take your milk blend and pour it on top of the cold brew, do not mix!

STEP 5: Sip and get back to work!

FOR A DASH OF MAGIC...

* For best results, make this on a Wednesday, which is ruled by Mercury, the planet of communication, learning, and understanding.

* This isn't just a study aid or a way to beat the 3 p.m. slump. This is great to sip if you need to focus on a big decision you need to make, stay sharp in an unfamiliar place, have an important conversation, or give your intuition a boost.

* The blue color of the milk can help open up your throat chakra.

RETROGRADE RX
A retrograde survival brew

Even if you don't follow astrology, you have probably heard about the dreaded Mercury in retrograde that seems to mess up most of our lives (or at least, that's how it feels). Mercury retrogrades affect our communication, interfere with our understanding, mess with technology, and can create plenty of delays. When the retrograde is in effect, here's a simple brew that can help get you through.

---

1 tablespoon lavender syrup (*happiness, healing, protection, relaxation, peace of mind*)

2 tablespoons medium roast ground coffee (*balance, flexibility, adaption, prosperity, strength, creativity, reliability, grounding, determination*). *Note: this makes one cup of coffee; if you want to make a pot of coffee, use more grounds.*

1 sprig fresh rosemary (*luck, intuition, cleansing, strength, protection, invigoration, memory*)

4 ounces streamed vanilla almond milk
(*mental quickness, wisdom, and luck*)

HOW TO BREW

STEP 1: Pour the lavender syrup into a mug.

STEP 2: Combine the ground coffee and the rosemary sprig together and add them in your coffee filter. For this recipe, an auto-drip coffee maker or a pour-over coffee maker works best. You can also use a French press with a teaspoon of ground rosemary.

STEP 3: Brew your coffee into your cup. Stir.

STEP 4: Froth your steamed milk, pour it into your mug, and stir. As you stir, say: "Bye-bye, retrograde. My life is moving forward with each sip." Sprinkle some dried lavender for garnish if desired.

STEP 5: Sip in a quiet place and enjoy this opportunity for pause and reflection.

FOR A DASH OF MAGIC...

This "Retrograde Rx" is best for Mercury's retrograde. To make this during Venus's retrograde, swap out the lavender syrup for rose syrup. For Mars's retrograde, swap out rosemary for ¼ teaspoon of cinnamon.

Sip this while using your coffee Zen garden for ultimate relaxation and calming your mind. See "A Moment to Get Grounded" on page 127.

If you need to journal your thoughts, do the coffee ink ritual ("Let Me Spell It Out for You") on page 129 while sipping this brew.

I NEED TO ESPRESSO MYSELF

For a boost of creativity

Coffee is the drink of choice among writers, artists, and creators. I'm drinking some as I write this! It's not hard to see why, magically speaking: Coffee removes energy blockages, brings focus, and increases our creativity and motivation. It also gives us a much-needed energy boost during a late-night creative season. However, as much as we all love creating, there's nothing worse than having a creative block, when all we want to do is express our thoughts but can't seem to put them into the right words. Fortunately, this magical drink can break through your blocks to help you create magic.

---

2 teaspoons instant espresso powder or 1 ounce brewed espresso (*energy, clarity, creativity, speed, productivity*)

1 tablespoon chocolate hazelnut spread (*magical energy replenishment, nurturing, grounding, balance, creativity, inspiration*)

1½ teaspoons sugar (*manifesting, multiplying*)

¼ teaspoon cinnamon (*success, energy, happiness, creativity*)

1/16 teaspoon ground cayenne pepper (*obstacle removal, speeding things up, road opener, cleansing, motivation, courage*)

1 cup oat milk (*grounding energy, increase in focus*)

HOW TO BREW

STEP 1: In your mug, stir in the espresso, chocolate hazelnut spread, sugar, and spices. Add in a few tablespoons of oat milk and mix into a paste.

STEP 2: Heat the rest of the milk in a saucepan on medium heat until hot. Pour your milk into the mug and stir clockwise.

STEP 3: As you stir, visualize yourself creating something. Whether you picture yourself writing, painting, sewing, whatever, visualize yourself doing that and doing it well, and that you are enjoying what you're creating!

STEP 4: Sip and get back to work!

FOR A DASH OF MAGIC...

※ For best results, brew this on a Wednesday. Wednesday is associated with Mercury, the planet of communication, learning, and creativity.

※ If you're writing or drawing, do the coffee ink ritual ("Let Me Spell It Out for You") on page 129 to help you slow down and think about what you want to put down on paper. This is also great for a rough draft.

※ Stir your drink with a cinnamon stick for an extra boost of creativity.

※ If you do creative work for a living, brew this coffee during your "Magic Morning Witch-ual" (page 96) to help start your day on a creative note.

※ To make your creativity come back faster, cast the "Let's Speed Things Along" spell (page 152) before starting the potion to help boost the energy of the potion.

EVERYTHING IS GOLDEN

To help you brew some golden opportunities into your life

We all need to use a little *magic* in our lives—an unexpected blessing, an opportunity that can change our life for the better. Something that can instantly boost our mood and our existence. While I won't promise that drinking this latte will utterly transform your life, everything may start looking a little more golden.

½ cup of almond milk (*wisdom, luck, prosperity*)

½ teaspoon honey (*sweetening of situations, magical energy replenishment, binding, love, kindness, wealth*)

¾ teaspoon ground turmeric (*protection, vitality, blessings, and golden opportunities*)

¼ teaspoon ground cinnamon (*luck, success, energy, happiness, psychic boost, protection, sun magic*)

¼ teaspoon ground ginger (*confidence, quick manifestation, energy boost, inner power, abundance, passion, balance, success, and retribution*)

1 teaspoon vanilla extract (*inner peace, happiness, luck, passion, positivity, vitality, mental quickness*)

1 ounce hot brewed espresso (*energy, clarity, awareness, speed, productivity*)

HOW TO BREW

STEP 1: In a saucepan, add your almond milk, honey, turmeric, cinnamon, ginger, and vanilla extract over medium heat.

STEP 2: Whisk clockwise when your mixture gets hot until the milk becomes foam. Take it off the heat.

STEP 3: While you're doing that, brew your espresso in your preferred way. Pour it into your mug.

STEP 4: Pour your frothed milk on top of your espresso and stir three times clockwise. As you stir, visualize your life filling with sunshine, that everything that can go right will go right. Say, "Everything that happens to me is golden."

STEP 5: Sip and enjoy!

MAGIC TRICKS

To make this recipe even easier, add the almond milk, honey, turmeric, cinnamon, ginger, and vanilla in a microwave-safe bowl. Microwave on high for about a minute. Then, use a milk frother or whisk until frothy. Pour the espresso into a cup and pour the milk mixture on top.

FOR A DASH OF MAGIC...

* Use a cinnamon stick when stirring in the magic for an extra boost of luck.

* Sip this brew when doing the "It's in the Bag" ritual on page 124.

* Before you sip, do the "Let's Speed Things Along" spell on page 152 before drinking to bring those golden opportunities faster.

* Use this brew to cast the "May Your Cup Runneth Over" spell on page 176.

RISE AND GRIND

A motivational coffee brew

Even the most productive witch needs a little help in the morning, when we simply *cannot* even deal with another day of work or trying to deal with the daily grind. Fortunately, when those days happen, pour yourself a cup of ambition and prepare for the rise and grind of everyday life.

———— ❖ ————

1 cup light roast coffee (*energy, clarity, motivation, abundance*)

1 cup oat milk (*determination and increase in focus*)

½ tablespoon molasses (*commitment, increase in drive, money, wisdom*)

½ teaspoon vanilla extract (*passion, strength, positivity, vitality, mental quickness*)

½ teaspoon cinnamon (*success, energy, happiness, creativity, money*)

¼ teaspoon ginger (*confidence, clarity, quick manifestation, energy boost, inner power, abundance, passion, success*)

¼ teaspoon allspice (*money, determination, and energy*)

———— ❖ ————

HOW TO BREW

STEP 1: Make your coffee the night before and let it chill in your refrigerator overnight.

STEP 2: That morning, mix your oat milk, molasses, vanilla extract, and spices in a blender and blend until frothed.

STEP 3: Pour the coffee into your to-go cup and pour the milk mixture over it. Stir and get ready for the day ahead.

MAGIC TRICKS

If you prefer hot coffee or black coffee in the morning, you can modify this brew into a hot Americano brew. Americano brings productivity, quickness, independence, strength, energy, and stability. Add some gingerbread syrup (homemade or store-bought) to the bottom of your cup, add in a tablespoon of instant espresso (energy, clarity, awareness, speed, productivity), and pour hot water over it.

FOR A DASH OF MAGIC...

Brew this coffee potion during your "Magic Morning Witch-ual" (page 96).

Hold a piece of carnelian stone while sipping this for a boost of motivation.

Drink while performing the "It's in the Bag" ritual on page 124 to help increase your motivation and make your manifestations appear faster.

BREW ME BACK TO LIFE
A healing brew

When most of us are feeling a little under the weather, we reach for tea to heal us. However, if you're not a big tea drinker or believe in the healing powers of coffee, here is a healing drink packed full of superfoods to help you feel good in no time at all.

MEDICAL NOTE: This drink is not a replacement for actual medical health. Please see a doctor or medical professional if you're not feeling well or experiencing a medical emergency.

---

2 tablespoons light roast coffee grounds *(energy healing)*

1 tablespoon cacao nibs *(magical energy replenishment, nurturing, grounding, balance, increase in emotional energy)*

1 teaspoon honey *(magical energy replenishment, healing, cleansing positivity, happiness, spirituality)*

½ teaspoon turmeric *(health, vitality, blessings)*

½ teaspoon vanilla extract *(inner peace, calm, strength, healing, comfort, vitality)*

¹⁄₁₆ teaspoon cayenne pepper *(removes obstacles, speeds things up, breaks hexes, cleansing, protection, strength)*

HOW TO BREW

STEP 1: Add the cacao nibs to your ground light roast coffee and brew to your liking.

STEP 2: When your coffee is brewed and in your mug, stir in the rest of your ingredients. Make sure you stir at least three times, clockwise, visualizing yourself feeling better again.

STEP 3: Sip and go back to bed—you need your rest!

FOR A DASH OF MAGIC...

※ For best results, brew this potion during the full moon, as it is best for healing spells and potions.

※ For best results, brew this potion on a Sunday, as it's ruled by the sun and is best for healing and strength spells.

※ Make your coffee using sun-charged water to infuse the healing powers of the sun.

※ Sip this before or after performing the "Chakra Me Back to Life" ritual on page 118 to help align your chakras so you can heal faster.

YOU MOCHA ME CRAZY
A bewitching love potion

Nothing brings people together quite like coffee. Meeting for coffee is a common first date for a reason. So, it only makes sense that a mocha is a perfect brew for a love potion. Here's a magical drink to inspire love eyes with every sip.

¾ cup half-and-half, or any milk *(nurturing and good vibes)*

2½ teaspoons granulated sugar *(attraction, love, manifesting, multiplying)*

1 tablespoon dried rose petals *(love, compassion)*

2 teaspoons raspberry syrup *(jubilation, commitment, confidence, attraction, love, strength, endurance, kindness, compassion, desire, sweetness, sex magic)*

2 ounces espresso *(energy, clarity, speed)*

1 cinnamon stick *(luck, success, energy, happiness, love magic)*

1 piece star anise *(happiness, dreams, falling in love)*

¼ teaspoon ground ginger *(confidence, sensuality, quick manifestation, energy boost, abundance, passion)*

1 tablespoon brown sugar *(sweetness, comfort, love)*

3 ounces chocolate *(love, increase in emotional energy, lust, binding)*

½ teaspoon vanilla extract *(love, happiness, lust, passion)*

whipped cream

chocolate sauce *(optional)*

NOTE: You can double the recipe to make it for two people.

HOW TO BREW

STEP 1: Mix your half-and-half, granulated sugar, rose petals, and raspberry syrup in a saucepan over low heat for 15 minutes. Stir occasionally.

STEP 2: When the 15 minutes are up, pour the rose-raspberry mixture through a mesh strainer and into a jar or bowl. Refrigerate until completely cooled.

STEP 3: In another small saucepan, heat your espresso, cinnamon stick, star anise, ground ginger, and brown sugar together and stir.

STEP 4: Cover your saucepan and bring it to a boil. Once it reaches a boil, put it on low heat and let it simmer for 10 minutes.

STEP 5: While that's simmering, chop up your chocolate and put it in the bottom of your mug. Add in the vanilla extract.

STEP 6: When your espresso mixture is finished simmering, remove the cinnamon stick and star anise.

STEP 7: Add the espresso mixture to the mug and stir, combining it with the chocolate and vanilla.

STEP 8: Take your rose-raspberry milk out of the fridge and steam it. Add to your coffee mug. Add whipped cream on top and chocolate sauce if desired.

STEP 9: Sip or give to your lover. Enjoy *wink*.

MAGIC TRICKS

✳ To simplify this recipe, use an auto-drip coffeemaker or pour over and mix your spices with your coffee grounds inside of using the saucepan.

FOR A DASH OF MAGIC...

✳ When making this spiced espresso, perform the "Just Like Magic" spell on page 154, saying what you want in a lover.

✳ For best results, make this brew on a Friday, as it's ruled by Venus, the planet of love and beauty.

✳ Make a love sigil using the chocolate sauce on top of your drink. See page 144 for "Sigil Magic."

✳ Sip this potion while performing a love tarot reading to help you find your perfect partner.

SPILLIN' THE BEANS

Love spells have been around for a long time and have been used in mocha-flavored drinks before. In Central America and Italy, a common love spell was to add menstrual blood to someone's coffee or hot chocolate. The other person drinks the liquid and becomes obsessed with that person. However, these were less of a "love" potion and more of a "lust" potion that sometimes had negative effects when the potion wore off.

CHANGING LEAVES, A CHANGE IN ME

A latte for the changes in life

Much like the seasons change, our lives go in different paths that we may not have originally envisioned for ourselves. We have to make tough choices and deal with obstacles that are outside of our control. When these things happen, it's easy to dig in our heels and stay stuck in the past. However, the wise thing, the brave thing, is to meet these changes head-on and allow ourselves to change and move into a new season. Here is a latte to help you move forward and move on.

---

1 tablespoon maple syrup (*learning, decision-making, dealing with change, spiritual healing, and adaptability*)

½ **tablespoon caramel** (*positivity transformation*)

⅛ **teaspoon ground cloves** (*protection, banishing negativity, courage*)

⅛ **teaspoon allspice** (*luck, healing, treasure, determination, and energy*)

⅛ **teaspoon nutmeg** (*luck, travel, lucid dreaming, attraction, psychic visions, getting justice*)

¼ **cup almond milk** (*wisdom, luck, prosperity*)

8 ounces medium roast coffee (*flexibility, adaption, strength, creativity, grounding, determination*)

HOW TO BREW

STEP 1: Add your maple syrup, caramel, and spices to your mug. Stir in a clockwise motion.

STEP 2: Pour your milk into a microwave-safe bowl and heat for thirty seconds. Whisk milk until foamy.

STEP 3: Pour your coffee into your mug and stir, clockwise. As you stir, visualize yourself at a fork in the road with two paths before you. Allow yourself to wonder about what each of those paths represents and what you are most drawn to.

STEP 4: Pour your milk foam in and drink. As you drink, think about the changes you need to make in your life and the actions you have to take.

FOR A DASH OF MAGIC...

- As maple represents travel, this is a great drink to use when doing the "Pour Me One for the Road" spell on page 165—especially if changes involved moving to a new place.
- Use the maple syrup to create a sigil on top of your drink. See "Sigil Magic" on page 144.

BERRY BREW-TI-FUL
A glamour brew

There are plenty of beauty hacks out there. It seems like every day there's a new viral trend that looks like it came straight out of a spell book. Well, whether these influencers realize it or not, they are participating in glamour magic. While glamour magic cannot make your nose different overnight or make you look exactly like your favorite celebrity, it can help bring out your natural beauty, boost your confidence, and attract people to you. Brew this altered flat white while you're getting ready or just want to embrace your natural beauty.

---

2 ounces espresso (*energy, clarity, awareness, creativity*)

½ cup frozen blueberries (*youthfulness, beauty*)

1 teaspoon lemon juice (*happiness, beauty, openness, clarity*)

2 tablespoons granulated sugar (*attraction, glamour, manifesting, multiplying*)

½ teaspoon water

¼ teaspoon rose water (*glamour*)

6 ounces coconut milk (*increases confidence*)

½ teaspoon vanilla extract (*inner peace, happiness, passion, positivity, vitality, beauty*)

HOW TO BREW

STEP 1: Brew two shots of espresso in your preferred way.

STEP 2: In a small saucepan, combine your blueberries, lemon juice, sugar, and water. Cook on medium heat and stir until the blueberries have broken down and the mixture has thickened.

STEP 3: Strain the mixture to remove blueberry seeds. Pour into a small bowl.

STEP 4: Stir in your rose water. Set the bowl aside.

STEP 5: Take your coconut milk and steam until frothy.

STEP 6: In a large mug, combine your steamed milk and espresso and stir clockwise. Add in your vanilla extract.

STEP 7: Spoon the blueberry-lemon-rose compote on top. Stir clockwise. As you stir, think about your best qualities, things you wish to highlight and want others to see. How do you want to look as you go through this life?

STEP 8: Sip and enjoy.

MAGIC TRICKS

For an easier way to brew this, use blueberry coffee and add in vanilla sugar and just a splash of rose water.

FOR A DASH OF MAGIC...

You can make a large batch of the blueberry-lemon-rose compote and keep it in your fridge for about a week. Use it in your "Magic Morning Witch-ual" (page 96) for a glamorous boost.

- Drink this coffee after performing the "Cleanse Me in Coffee" ritual on page 116 to show off your natural beauty after cleansing yourself.

- Drink this coffee after performing the "Chakra Me Back to Life" ritual on page 118 as part of your beauty and spiritual treatment.

- Draw a sigil for glamour, beauty, attraction, or confidence on the top of your drink using a latte art pen (see "Draw Me a Spell" on page 147).

APPLE OF MY AFFOGATO
A gratitude spell that satisfies

"Gratitude" is increasingly becoming a buzzword in wellness space—how to practice gratitude and acknowledging the things you are grateful for in your life. While it's great to acknowledge what you have going right in your life and to savor each moment, sometimes it can be hard to see the silver lining. Here is a fun brew that reminds you that every day is a sweet gift.

---

1 ounce espresso (*energy, clarity, protection, awareness, creativity, productivity*)

2 scoops vanilla ice cream (*inner peace, happiness, passion, friendship, calm, positivity, comfort*)

1 teaspoon ground cinnamon (*luck, success, happiness, psychic boost*)

1 tablespoon apple butter (*gratitude, generosity, creativity, abundance*)

1 tablespoon caramel (*positivity, comfort, memory, self-love, soothing*)

HOW TO BREW

STEP 1: Brew your espresso shot to your liking.

STEP 2: Put your vanilla ice cream into a bowl. Add the cinnamon on top.

STEP 3: Pour the espresso on top of your ice cream. As you pour, think of yourself pouring hope, trust, and gratitude all over the negative parts of your life. Focus on the good.

STEP 4: Drizzle your apple butter and caramel sauce on top.

STEP 5: Enjoy! With each spoonful, write down something that you're grateful for.

MAGIC TRICK

Replace the espresso with apple-flavored coffee or replace the vanilla ice cream with apple-flavored ice cream.

FOR A DASH OF MAGIC...

Replace the apple butter with the apple syrup from "Piece of the Pie" (page 60) for an extra boost of abundance (and to bring you something that you'll really be grateful for).

Eat this before writing out the things you are grateful for in coffee ink (from the "Let Me Spell It Out for You" ritual on page 129).

Make this potion after performing the "It's in the Bag" ritual on page 124 to show gratitude for what you may receive from the universe.

WHEN LIFE GIVES YOU LEMONS
A potion for turning the sour to sweet

Life happens, even to the best of witches. We are often faced with struggles and issues that can leave a sour taste in our mouth as we search for a way to overcome. However, while it's tempting to stay sour, we can easily transform our problems into wonderful gifts. Here's a potion to give you a mood boost, even when the world burns around you. Kidding… kind of…

½ cup vanilla cold brew coffee *(intuition, balance, level-headedness and impartiality, inner peace, happiness, luck, calm, strength, positivity, comfort, vitality)*

½ cup raspberries *(faith, confidence, attraction, protection, strength, endurance, kindness, compassion, sweetness, reliability)*

½ cup sugar *(attraction, manifesting, smoothing things over, multiplying)*

1 cup coconut milk *(confidence, spirituality, protection)*

ice *(optional)*

½ cup of lemonade *(purification, happiness, longevity, openness, removal of hexes, clarity, sun magic)*

½ teaspoon sun-infused water *(happiness, positivity, energy)*

HOW TO BREW

STEP 1: Brew your vanilla-infused cold brew. You can either purchase vanilla cold brew already made or make your own cold brew by using vanilla-infused coffee beans.

STEP 2: Make your raspberry cold foam. First, put your raspberries in a saucepan and heat at a low temperature.

STEP 3: When the raspberries start to liquefy, add in your sugar and stir. Let cook for 4 minutes.

STEP 4: Remove your raspberries from the heat and put them through a strainer to remove the seeds.

STEP 5: Pour your coconut milk into a jug, stir in your raspberry mixture until well combined.

STEP 6: Froth the milk mixture until you get to your desired texture.

STEP 7: Take a glass and fill it with ice.

STEP 8: Pour your cold brew and lemonade into the glass and stir to combine. Add in your sun water.

STEP 9: Take your cold foam and pour it on top.

STEP 10: Sip and enjoy your day.

MAGIC TRICKS

※ You can also use the raspberry-rose syrup from "You Mocha Me Crazy" brew on page 75 and add to your milk, especially if you're looking to become lucky in love again.

FOR A DASH OF MAGIC...

※ Draw sigils for positivity and happiness in the raspberry cold foam (see "Sigil Magic" on page 144).

※ If you wish to speed up the good vibes, cast the "Let's Speed Things Along" spell (page 152) on the brew before drinking.

RISK IS THE SPICE OF LIFE
A bravery brew

Let's face it, the world can be a pretty scary place. And if you're an overthinker like me, your mind makes it an even scarier place, always looking at the worst-case scenarios. When anxiety takes the wheel, we can easily talk ourselves out of things that may have improved our lives and made us happier. This brew is a little shot of confidence to help soothe our worried minds and provide the courage to try new things. This isn't a spell to disregard safety but to help us choose life over fear.

---

1 shot espresso (energy, protection, productivity)

1 cup cashew milk (strength)

⅛ teaspoon ground allspice (luck, determination, and energy)

⅛ teaspoon ground nutmeg (luck, travel, attraction, psychic visions, prosperity)

3 cardamom pods (clarity, courage, direction, wisdom)

1 tablespoon molasses (overcome enemies, stick to situations, increases drive, wisdom, and business success)

¼ teaspoon cinnamon and one cinnamon stick (luck, success, energy, happiness, psychic boost, protection, love magic)

HOW TO BREW

STEP 1: Brew a shot of espresso however you want. Put it aside to cool.

STEP 2: In a small saucepan, add half of your milk and all of your spices and heat until steaming.

STEP 3: In your mug, mix your espresso and molasses.

STEP 4: Strain your spiced milk to remove the cardamom pods.

STEP 5: Make the rest of your cashew milk foam using your preferred methods.

STEP 6: Pour your steamed milk into your espresso mug and stir with your cinnamon stick. As you stir clockwise say, "Every time I act with courage, I grow into the person I'm supposed to become" three times.

STEP 7: Pour your milk foam on top of your drink and add a pinch of cinnamon on top.

STEP 8: Drink and get ready for your adventures!

FOR A DASH OF MAGIC...

* Brew this coffee blend right before you have to make a big life change or before taking a big risk.

* For best results, drink this on a Tuesday. Tuesday is ruled by Mars, the warrior planet of bravery.

* Draw sigils of bravery, courage, and fearlessness in the foam (see "Sigil Magic" on page 144).

* You can transform this brew into a spell jar by adding smaller amounts of espresso, allspice, nutmeg, cinnamon, and cardamom into a small jar. Carry it with you in your bag, place it on your desk, or wear it as a necklace. Keep this close to give you a boost of bravery wherever you go.

COFFEE PROTECT ME

A protective brew

As I mentioned in the last potion, we all need to take a risk every now and again. However, sometimes we need to accept that the world *is* a scary place, and we need to protect ourselves as such. From keeping that creep at the coffee shop as far away as possible to brewing when you are staying alone at a new place for the first time, this brew is great to travel with to give you an extra boost of protection. While this potion doesn't replace actual safety measures (locking your doors, not talking to strangers, asking for help when you need it), it can offer a little extra layer of magical protection.

---

1 ounce espresso (*protection, banishment, awareness, curse casting, curse breaking*)

1 teaspoon real maple syrup (*travel, decision-making, protection, adaptability*)

1 sprig fresh rosemary (*intuition, strength, protection*)

3 peppermint leaves or ⅛ teaspoon peppermint extract (*positive thoughts, cleansing, speaking up, protection*)

1 cup soy milk (*protection*)

HOW TO BREW

STEP 1: Brew your espresso shot and set it aside for later.

STEP 2: In a saucepan, heat up your maple syrup, rosemary, and peppermint for about 2 minutes. Then, remove from heat and strain out the herbs using a mesh strainer.

STEP 3: Combine your espresso with your maple mixture in your coffee cup.

STEP 4: Steam your soy milk and pour it over your coffee. Stir three times clockwise. As you stir, say: "With each sip I am protected. No harm shall come to me. My aura is strong. Nothing can slip through it."

STEP 5: Drizzle the maple syrup mixture on the top. Sip and stay safe.

FOR A DASH OF MAGIC...

- If you want to use this brew to banish negative energy or a negative person, add two whole cloves to your maple mixture to banish bad vibes.

- Use the maple syrup to write a sigil for safety or protection (see "Sigil Magic" on page 144).

- Perform the "Pour Me One for the Road" spell on page 165 on this coffee for safety and protection in your travels, especially if you're going alone to a place you've never been before.

- Drink this after casting the "Get the Hex Out" spell on page 183 for extra protection.

Chapter 3

BREWING UP SOME MAGIC RITUALS

☾ ☾ ✳ ☽ ☽

Ingredients alone are only part of the reason why coffee is so magical. The rituals that go along with the ingredients also make coffee so sacred to our lives—from those quiet moments in the morning when no one is up and you make that first pot of the day, to grabbing a latte with a friend every Thursday as a chance to stay connected. Whether you have a long and complex method of making "the perfect cup of coffee," simply press the "brew" button on a machine, or grab a cup on the way to work, you are creating a daily ritual for yourself. The magic comes by adding intention to these rituals. When you stir cinnamon into your morning coffee, do you realize that you're stirring in luck and success? When you make a mocha for your partner every evening, do you know you're infusing your love into the brew? In this chapter, we'll present all the coffee magic rituals you can do. Whether you're searching for the answer to your most burning questions at the bottom of your cup or want to add a little magic to your daily brew, there's a ritual for you.

COFFEE BAR ALTAR
A magical place to brew your potions and spells

An altar is a sacred space that acts as a reflection of your magical self. Altars can be used as a place to practice magic or meditate, they can be used as a place where we put our magical tools, or they can act as spells that manifest in our home and serve as a reminder of what we are trying to bring to life. Altars can come in all forms, from being a focal point in your home decorating to something you can carry with you on the go. Since you'll be spending time brewing up coffee potions and conjuring up spells, it only makes sense that you make your workstation a magical place. Here's how you can turn your home coffee bar into a functional altar.

---

a table or counter space

altar cloth/table runner

your coffee tools (*coffee maker, espresso machine, French press, milk frother, etc.; whatever you use to make coffee*)

coffee ingredients (*coffee grounds, coffee beans, coffee pods, powder creamers, espresso powder, sugars, syrups, etc.; whatever you add to your coffee that doesn't have to be refrigerated*)

spoon(s)

mugs

mug organizer

glass jars/bottles/canisters

storage organizer/shelves

mortar and pestle

tarot cards

crystals *(use any you like but I recommend carnelian for vitality and creativity, clear quartz for peace and cleansing, black tourmaline for protection, and citrine for happiness)*

trinket dish/mini cauldron

plants/flowers

felt letter board

recipe books *(like this one!)*

FOR CLEANSING SPRAY

empty spray bottle

fresh water, enough to fill the bottle *(preferably charged with clear quartz)*

a sprig of rosemary *(cleansing and protection)*

4 drops of lemon essential oil *(purification, openness, clarity, removal of hexes)*

NOTE: The majority of items on this list are merely suggestions, so please don't feel the need to create a completely new setup in your kitchen or buy things to make it "witchy." At the end of the day, put together a space that feels right to you.

THE RITUAL

STEP 1: Wipe down your table or counter space. Make sure everything is nice and clean. Ideally, you should clean up your coffee station every three months to keep your energy fresh and your coffee area sanitary.

STEP 2: Make your cleansing spray by adding water, rosemary, and lemon essential oil. Spray the area around your altar. This is a great way to cleanse the energy around your space and make sure there is no lingering negative energy. Leave this spray in the fridge to keep it fresh.

STEP 3: Place your coffee tools, ingredients, spoon(s), and mugs on your altar. Play around with this setup to figure out what makes sense to you. Just make sure the space isn't too cluttered so you don't get overwhelmed. Utilize things like a storage shelf, organizers, and glass jars and bottles to make everything neat and put together. You can also place your recipe books and other witchcraft books there for quick access.

And those are the basics of setting up your coffee altar. If you want to give it a more witchy twist, read below.

FOR A DASH OF MAGIC...

- Place your tarot or oracle deck on the altar in its own special place, either in a trinket dish or its own bag. Place coffee beans around the cards to charge their energy and cleanse them so they are ready for use.

- Use a long altar cloth as a table runner on your coffee bar. You can make your own by picking up some witchy fabric at your local craft store and sewing it together. You can also pick up a table runner that you like, whatever feels magical to you and fits the vibe you're trying to achieve for your altar.

- Place crystals such as the ones listed above around your altar to help charge your area with the intentions you want to bring to your coffee. You can keep and reuse the same crystals or change them out depending on your intentions for the day.

- Place a piece of clear quartz in your mug overnight to charge the mug. This is perfect if you're doing a potion or a divination reading in that mug.

- Keep a mortar and pestle on your altar to grind up your ingredients when making a brew or casting a spell. This helps infuse your personal energy into the ingredients before using.

- For a witchy aesthetic, pour your ingredients into potion bottles and cauldrons. You can usually get these on sale right before and after Halloween.

- If you have the space, put some plants on your altar for extra positive energy and a symbol of growth. You can sprinkle some coffee grounds on your plants as well (see "From the Grounds Up" spell on page 159).

- Add a felt letter board to your altar with the "brew of the day" written on it or a positive affirmation to get your day (or night) started on the right note.

- Place some dried flowers upside down with the corresponding magic intention you desire to bring that energy into your space. For example, hang some dried roses for love, glamour, and psychic abilities.

MAGIC MORNING WITCH-UAL: A MAGICAL WAY TO START THE DAY

That first cup of coffee of the day is a magical thing. It can set the tone for your whole day. However, because of how hectic and chaotic daily life can be, we rarely have time to enjoy our coffee, usually gulping it down as we run off from place to place, crisis to crisis. Soon our morning ritual just becomes another chore we have to get through in order to make it to the next task on our never-ending to-do list. This ritual will help bring you back to the present and add the magic of mindfulness before you start your day.

---

your favorite morning coffee (*you can also use one of the coffee recipes from Chapter Two*)

your favorite coffee mug (*or a mug that feels super witchy*)

whatever milk, sugar, and creamer you typically use (*if you prefer your coffee black, that's perfectly fine!*)

one cinnamon stick (*optional, but brings success, happiness, protection, energy, and a psychic boost*)

a spoon

a crystal (*also optional, but I recommend citrine as it brings energy and motivation*)

THE RITUAL

STEP 1: Make your coffee. You can use any method you like and any kind of coffee you like. Do each step deliberately and thoughtfully. Don't just press a button on your machine and move on, go through each step of the process with clear intentions. When you pour in your creamer, pour in your hopes for the day. When you think about the machine heating up your water, think about your own passions rising within you. What are you hoping this day will bring you? Pour your coffee into your favorite mug when it's brewed.

STEP 2: Take your mug and sit down in a chair, feet firmly on the ground. Hold the mug in both hands and really feel the heat coming from it. If you have a cold coffee, feel the chill coming from it. Think of this as your connection to the brew. The energy from the coffee is flowing into you. Soak it in.

STEP 3: Look into the surface of the coffee and allow yourself to stare into it for a moment and visualize your day. Imagine your day going well and everything going the best way possible way.

STEP 4: Take your cinnamon stick (or spoon) and stir your coffee three times clockwise with it. Aloud or in your mind, say: "The magic is within me. With each sip, I feel the magic bright within me."

STEP 5: Sip your coffee. Don't just try to get it down as fast as possible. Be slow and mindful about each sip. If you are having breakfast with it, savor your food. This is also a great time to do a tarot card reading, do some journaling or planning, or simply hold your crystal and sit with your thoughts.

STEP 6: When you have only a sip left, take a moment to make a wish. Not a big wish like "I wish I'd win a million dollars" or "I wish to meet the love of my life today." Make it a small wish, something that could happen today. Something like "I hope my date goes well," or "I hope I get good news at work today," or even "I hope the place I'm going for lunch has my favorite brownie." Make it small but hopeful.

STEP 7: Take that last sip and start your day.

FOR A DASH OF MAGIC...

❋ Keep a piece of clear quartz (for cleansing) or a crystal of your choice at the bottom of your cup overnight. The magic properties of the crystals will infuse into your cup, charging it with the energy of the crystal. Just make sure to take it out before you put the coffee in.

❋ Do this ritual with the "Coffee and Cards" ritual on page 107, if you want to start your day with a tarot reading.

❋ Do this ritual with "Are You Seer-ing This?" on page 111 to get a glimpse of what the day may bring.

❋ Do this ritual with the "Just Like Magic" spell on page 154 to add a little magical boost to your day.

❋ If you have time in the morning, perform "Draw Me a Spell" sigil art spell on page 147.

❋ Drink the "Peppermint Perk Up" from page 53 to add a little boost to start your day.

❋ Make a coffee candle from the "A Cup Full of Light" ritual on page 132 to start your day with a candle burning or to just have a lovely candle at your altar.

FORTUNE IN YOUR CUP
A coffee divination reading

Tasseography is the divination method of reading the patterns of leaves, grounds, and sediments at the bottom of a cup to interpret the future. While we mainly associate tasseography with tea, reading coffee grounds is quite popular, especially in Greece and Turkey. In fact, the origins of tasseography began not with tea but with coffee, first appearing in the Ottoman palaces in the 1500s. It was called "Fal," which translates to "fortune." Fal is still a tradition practiced in Turkish culture, where it acts as more of a social activity. Friends and loved ones would gather around and read each other's cups to divine each other's future and give advice.

While we usually try to avoid grounds in our coffee, this ritual will help us brew up Turkish coffee (or something similar to it) and read our fortunes.

SPILLIN' THE BEANS

According to Turkish tradition, drinking one cup of coffee together guarantees many years of friendship.

---

a small cooking pot *(or Turkish coffeepot)*
1 cup water

2 tablespoons Turkish ground coffee *(you can buy this at a specialty store or buy regular coffee beans and grind them very finely)*

granulated sugar, to taste *(optional, but Turkish coffee is more bitter than your regular brew)*

a white teacup

a small saucer or plate

friends *(optional)*

— ❖ —

NOTE: The measurements listed here are for one cup of coffee. If you're making this for multiple people, you will have to add more coffee grounds and water. The ratio is that for every eight ounces of water, you should add one to two tablespoons of coffee, but go according to your taste.

THE RITUAL

STEP 1: Place your pot on the stovetop and turn the burner to medium heat. You can also use a cezve (a traditional Turkish coffeepot that has a wide bottom and is made of copper), however, your instructions will be a little different (see note).

STEP 2: Pour the water into your pot and bring it to a boil.

STEP 3: Add a big tablespoon of ground coffee to the water. If you wish to add sugar, add it now. Stir the liquid.

NOTE: if you're using a cezve, add the water, coffee, and sugar at the same time and then bring to a boil.

STEP 4: Turn off the stove's heat and let the pot rest for 3 minutes, stirring occasionally to keep the grounds moving. Taste your coffee to see if you need to add more coffee or sugar.

STEP 5: Pour the liquid into your cup. If grounds have settled to the bottom of your pot, simply add a spoonful of grounds from the pot to your cup.

STEP 6: Continue to sip your coffee from the same side of the cup. Take your time when drinking. Chat with your friends, read a book, or just mindfully enjoy each sip.

STEP 7: When there is about one sip left of the coffee, swirl the liquid around in your cup using your left hand so the grounds are loose.

STEP 8: Take the last sip and make a wish.

STEP 9: Place your saucer over the top of your cup.

STEP 10: Flip your coffee cup and saucer upside down. Take the handle of your cup with your left hand and swirl it around the plate three times, going clockwise.

STEP 11: Leave the cup for about 7 minutes, giving the cup a chance to cool and your pattern to form. If this reading is about money, put a coin on the cup. If this reading is about relationships, place a ring on the cup.

THE READING

In this section, we'll be discussing how to read your cup. Traditionally, coffee readings were done in groups with friends and/or loved ones reading each other's cups. However, you can easily do a coffee reading on your own. For this section, I will be referring to "the reader" as whoever is reading the cup and the "cup's owner" as whoever has been drinking from that cup.

STEP 1: When the cup is cool, the reader will slowly lift the cup from the saucer and hold it upright.

STEP 2: There are many ways to interpret a cup reading, depending on the theme of the question and what the grounds in the cup look like. In this book, we'll be showing you two different ways to read a cup.

READING 1

Divide the cup into five sections in your mind. Each section represents a different area of life. The cup should be divided like this:

- ✴ **Handle side:** Love and romantic relationships and friendships
- ✴ **Front rim (directly opposite of the handle):** Money matters
- ✴ **Bottom of the cup:** Home life and family relationships
- ✴ **Sip side (part of the cup that was sipped from):** Current situation
- ✴ **Lower rim (directly opposite of the sip side):** The future

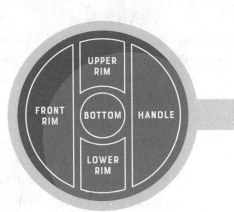

Once the reader has divided up the cup, they can take note of what they see. If any symbols, letters, numbers, or feelings come up, the reader should feel free to say them out loud to the owner or write them down. Some of these symbols can be personal and unique to the cup owner. For example, the reader may see a dog paw in the bottom of the cup, and the cup owner may have a new puppy at home or is thinking of getting a dog. Or the symbols could be more abstract to the owner, like a bird or an apple. Feel free to consult a dream journal or website to help understand these symbols.

The reader should feel free to ask the cup owner questions throughout the reading as it can help make sense of the reading and tell a more accurate story of the future. If the meaning isn't quite clear to the reader, they can write down what they see and use it to look back on later with a fresh set of eyes.

READING 2

For those new to tasseography or having trouble dividing the cup mentally in their mind, this reading allows you to see into the future by looking at the grounds as a whole instead of trying to find symbols within.

✴ **If the whole cup is covered in a thin layer of grounds:** The cup owner is stretching themselves too thin in all areas of their life, trying to be everywhere at once and burning themselves out. They need to learn to let go of control.

✴ **If the grounds are spread evenly throughout the whole cup:** The cup owner's destiny is in their hands. While life is about to get pretty busy and a little intense, it's nothing they can't handle. These will be good changes and the cup owner is more than ready for them.

✴ **If the grounds are spread unevenly throughout the cup:** Not a great sign, as things are going to be a little rocky. The cup owner has a lot on their plate (or saucer) that's causing a great deal of anxiety. Something has to give.

✴ **If the grounds are spread in a chaotic way:** Yikes! Something is up in the cup owner's life that is causing major stress and perhaps spelling disaster. They need to piece themselves together!

✴ **If the grounds look smudged:** There is a lot of uncertainty in the cup owner's life. Their path can go in many different directions as they feel a lack of direction. The cup owner is very unsure of themself right now. They need to make a decision about something important.

- **Mostly dark grounds:** Important events are coming, but the cup owner is strong enough to handle them. Positive changes are on their way.

- **Mostly light grounds:** This indicates a turning point in the cup owner's life that can be very stressful. They need to solve problems quickly and productively.

- **Mixed-colored grounds:** The cup holder has some hidden stress in their lives that they are not addressing. They need to balance the positive and the negative.

- **Blobs of grounds at the bottom of the cup:** The cup owner is struggling with self-doubt.

- **The bottom of the cup is covered in a thick layer of grounds:** The cup holder is a strong, courageous person who can handle anything.

- **The bottom of the cup is covered in a thin layer of grounds:** The cup holder is holding on by a thread. They may seem to have it together, but they are completely avoiding their problems.

- **The grounds are split into two pieces at the bottom of the cup:** The cup reader has found freedom. They are getting their independence back in every aspect of their lives. It may not be pretty, but it'll be worth it.

- **No grounds at the bottom of the cup:** The cup holder is having a tough time right now. They need to remember to stay positive and find a support system.

FOR A DASH OF MAGIC...

For more ideas on how to divide your cup, read *Herbal Tea Magic for the Modern Witch*, which has a whole chapter on tea reading rituals that can easily be adapted to coffee readings.

Before doing the coffee reading, perform the "Are You Seering This?" ritual on page 111 to gaze into your future. You can even compare notes from the scrying and the grounds reading.

Need some clarity on your reading? Pull a tarot or oracle card for guidance. Check out "Coffee and Cards" on the next page for more details.

COFFEE AND CARDS
A tarot reading

Is there a more iconic duo than coffee and tarot cards? Not when it comes to magic. There's nothing I love more than pouring a cup of coffee and doing a tarot reading. Cartomancy is probably one of the most recognizable forms of divination and one of the most popular with witches, fortune-tellers, and woo-curious alike. For those a little unfamiliar with the fancy title, cartomancy is the art of divination using a deck of cards to gain insight into future events, as well as understanding the past. This includes tarot, oracle decks, Lenormand, and even playing cards. Here's a spread that blends coffee and cards together to see into the future.

---

a cup of coffee

a tarot deck *(or any type of deck you wish)*

a flat surface

pen and paper *(optional)*

THE RITUAL

STEP 1: Make your cup of coffee to your liking and sit down.

STEP 2: Shuffle your deck. As you shuffle, think about the day ahead (or the next day if you're doing this at night). Put all your energy into the cards as you shuffle. When you're ready, pull four cards, facedown, and put them in a spread like this:

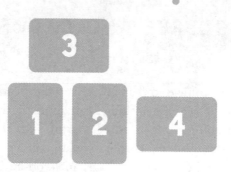

* **Card 1:** Grounds: What is grounding me?
* **Card 2:** Heat: What are the energy and events that will drive me?
* **Card 3:** Aroma: Where can I find pleasure?
* **Card 4:** Energy: What will keep me going?

STEP 3: Flip the cards over and do your reading. Use your pen and paper (or the notes app on your phone) to record your thoughts. Sip your coffee and really think about the meaning of each card. (If you are new to tarot, look up the meaning online or in a tarot book.)

If you have a tarot deck and would like to do another spread, try this one that invokes the four elements of coffee.

STEP 1: In your tarot deck, separate your minor arcana into four stacks: one stack is the suit of swords, one stack is the suit of wands, one stack is the suit of cups, and one stack is the suit of pentacles.

NOTE: Since tarot card decks do vary slightly, the exact names of your suits may be different; names like "pentacles" may be called "coins," or "cups" may be renamed "chalices." Either way, you should have four suits, all representing elements similar to the original suits.

STEP 2: When you're ready, shuffle each deck separately. Once each stack is shuffled, pull the top card from each, facedown, and put all four on the spread like this:

- ✷ **Card 1:** Earth (the pentacles suit): Where are you standing on this issue/what does your body want you to know?
- ✷ **Card 2:** Fire (the wands suit): What action do you need to take/what should you focus on?
- ✷ **Card 3:** Water (the cups suit): Where you are emotionally?
- ✷ **Card 4:** Air (the swords suit): What approach do you need to take?

STEP 3: Flip the cards over and do your reading. Write notes using your pen and paper or notes app. Sip your coffee and think about the meaning of each card and its potential meaning for your situation. (If you are new to tarot, look up the meaning online or in a tarot book.)

FOR A DASH OF MAGIC...

✷ Put coffee beans in the same place you store your deck. Coffee beans can cleanse your cards of any negative energy that comes from a heavy reading and add a shot of positive energy to the deck for your next reading.

This is a great ritual to do alongside your "Magic Morning Witch-ual" (page 96). You can also do a one-card pull to get a read on your upcoming day to keep things simple.

Do this reading along with your "Fortune in Your Cup" reading (page 99) to get a deeper divination and perhaps more clarity on your future.

When doing a coffee divination reading, you can divide your cup the same way you would a three-card reading. For example, if doing a past, present, and future reading, the rim would be the past, the present would be the middle of your cup, and the future would be the bottom of your cup. Do this for any of your favorite three-card spreads.

You can also do the "Are you Seer-ing This?" ritual (page 111) before you start your tarot reading to help you get a glimpse of your future.

Sip the "Red Eye for the Third Eye" brew (page 51) to help awaken your intuition.

Perform the sigil latte foam art on your coffee to boost your intuition and psychic intuition (page 144 for "Sigil Magic").

ARE YOU SEER-ING THIS?
A coffee scrying ritual

Have you ever looked into your coffee just a little bit too long and your mind started drifting? You may be getting a psychic vision, thanks to scrying. Scrying is a form of divination that uses a reflective surface to tell the future. This can be a crystal ball, a pool of water, or your own cup of coffee. Here's a simple ritual that can help us see into the future as we get ready for our day.

---

dark roast coffee (*meditation, divination, accuracy*)

a black mug that is also black on the inside

a quiet place to think

a spoon

a notebook and pen

a pendulum (*optional*)

THE RITUAL

STEP 1: Prepare your dark roast coffee in your preferred method. You'll need to drink this coffee black to get the best result. If you simply cannot drink black coffee, wait until the end of the ritual to prepare your coffee to your liking.

STEP 2: Pour your coffee into the black mug. Take your drink to a quiet place. This is an ideal ritual to do either early in the morning or at night.

STEP 3: When you are settled in, take your spoon and stir your drink clockwise three times. Watch the liquid swirl in your cup. Don't try to think about any particular question or any outcome. Just let it swirl and let your mind relax.

STEP 4: Wait for the liquid to go completely still and stare into it, allowing your mind to wander. This could take several minutes so do not rush it. As you allow your focus to drift, take note of anything you see in your cup. What do you see on the surface? What about the steam floating from the cup? Are there any particular shapes? Consider everything.

STEP 5: When you're ready, take your eyes away from the cup and write down in your notebook everything you've seen. Just jot it down without thinking too much about it. When you're finished writing, take in the meaning of everything.

STEP 6: Drink the rest of your coffee as you meditate on what you saw. If you don't understand some of the symbolism of what you've seen, consult a dream dictionary for guidance.

FOR A DASH OF MAGIC...

* If you have a pendulum, place it over your brew and start asking questions. If the pendulum swings left, the answer is no. If the pendulum swings right, it's a yes. If the pendulum swings up and down, it's yes. If a pendulum swings back and forth, it's no). You can also tie a piece of star anise to a string and use that as a pendulum.

* Use the "Red Eye for the Third Eye" brew on page 51 for a boost of intuition and psychic boost.

* For best results, perform this during the waning crescent moon, which is the ideal time for scrying.

CLOUDS IN MY COFFEE
A milk foam reading

Have you ever gotten so focused on doing a task that you kind of zone out, your mind getting so clear that you can suddenly work out a problem that you have been struggling with? Maybe the answer or a clue about your future has been standing in front of you the whole time? Or floating on the top of your coffee. For this ritual, we'll be making a traditional macchiato, a brew associated with spells, movement, and catalysts, and decoding the future by looking at the coffee cloud within.

---❖---

1 shot espresso

a small cup

1 ounce milk *(whole milk or oat milk*

a milk frother pitcher *(or a cup)*

a milk frother *(or French press or whisk)*

a spoon

pen and paper *(optional)*

sprinkle of cinnamon *(optional)*

---❖---

THE RITUAL

STEP 1: Take a deep breath and cleanse your mind. Exhale any worries or negative feelings you are currently having and leave your mind open and accepting as you work.

STEP 2: Make your espresso the way you normally prepare it. If you don't have espresso, you can use 1½ ounces of strong dark roast coffee. Pour into your cup.

STEP 3: Heat up your milk either on the stovetop, microwave, or using the steamer on the espresso maker. The milk should be hot but not boiling.

STEP 4: Pour your milk into your pitcher or cup. Use your milk frother (or whatever you use to froth the milk) to froth the milk. You want to make this a light and fluffy foam. As you froth, think about the question you have in mind for the reading or the vibes you are currently feeling.

STEP 5: When your milk is nice and fluffy, with your spoon, remove the top of the foam from the milk. Place that dollop of milk right on top of your espresso. Ask your question, if you have one.

STEP 6: Study the milk cloud in your coffee. What does it look like? Does its shape remind you of anything? Make a note of everything you see, even if you don't think it's important right now. If you don't see any particular shape (other than a blob of milk foam), here are some things to look out for:

- ✶ **If the milk foam is in a perfect circle:** Your life is in perfect balance. Everything is working out for your higher purpose.

- ✶ **If the milk foam has jagged edges:** You're going through a rough spot. The future is unclear.

- ✶ **If the milk cloud is small:** Narrow-mindedness is blocking you from your goal.

- ✶ **If the milk cloud is too large:** You're letting your problems get the best of you. It's not that deep!

- ✶ **If the milk foam is thin:** You're feeling stressed due to financial loss.
- ✶ **If the milk foam is thick:** Money is coming your way.
- ✶ **If the milk foam has a high peak:** You are reaching your goals soon, feeling very accomplished.
- ✶ **If the milk foam has an indentation in the middle:** Look into your heart to find the source of your problem and the solution.
- ✶ **If the milk foam has little droplets next to it:** Ask your loved ones to help you. Or, give support to your loved ones.
- ✶ **If your espresso mixes in with your milk foam:** Love is coming your way.

For any shapes that you see, like a heart or a triangle, for example, consult a dream dictionary.

- ✶ **If the milk foam is near the edge of your cup:** Your problems will be solved soon.

STEP 7: Sip and meditate on both your question and answer.

FOR A DASH OF MAGIC...

- ✸ Add a sprinkle of cinnamon (psychic boost) or nutmeg (psychic vision) to help strengthen your intuition and make the changes to your foam a little more obvious—especially if you're reading for the first time.
- ✸ For best results, perform this ritual during the new moon, as it is optimal for performing divination practices.
- ✸ For best results, perform this ritual on a Monday, as it is ruled by the moon and associated with divination and spirituality.

CLEANSE ME IN COFFEE
A negativity-releasing coffee bath

Sure, we all know that coffee is great to drink, but did you know that you can bathe in coffee as well? Taking a coffee bath can help you wash away all of the negativity of the day, get rid of the bad vibes, and renew your emotional and spiritual energies.

---

white candles

clear quartz *(optional)*

2 cups strong brewed coffee *(cleansing, grounding, removing energy blockage, boosting stamina and motivation, clarity)*

2 cups Epsom salt *(cleansing, protection, clarity)*

a squeeze of fresh lemon *(healing, cleansing, vitality)*

THE RITUAL

STEP 1: Prepare your bath as you would normally do. Light your white candles, as white is associated with cleansing and healing. Take a deep breath to ground yourself. Place clear quartz around your tub, if you wish, and turn on your music.

STEP 2: Once the water is hot enough for your liking, pour in the coffee and Epsom salt. Mix it all into the water. Squeeze the lemon into the water. As you mix the water around, say: "I am letting go of the negativity that clings to my skin. I will wash away the stress and the frustration and come out clean."

STEP 3: When you're ready, step into the bath, and say out loud: "I will not come out of this bath the same person. When I leave this tub, my aura will be fresh, clean, and brand new."

STEP 4: Take your bath and allow yourself to wash away all the stress and tension from the day. Don't think about it. Turn your attention to happier things and let the coffee bath do the work. However, do not stay in the bath longer than 15 minutes as it has the potential to stain the skin.

STEP 5: Get out of the bath and drain the tub. As you watch the coffee water go down the drain, visualize all the negative energy going down with it.

FOR A DASH OF MAGIC...

- If you're looking for some extra energy in your coffee bath, add a teaspoon of espresso powder into the bath. If you need more grounding energy, use decaf coffee instead of regular.

- If you don't want to take a whole bath filled with coffee, take a coffee footbath by putting coffee, Epsom salt, and lemon juice into a bucket and soaking your feet for fifteen minutes. The feet are associated with the root chakra, which is the entry point into cleansing your whole-body system.

- For extra cleansing and relaxation, use lavender-infused Epsom salts to get those relaxing, healing vibes.

- Use vanilla-scented body lotion to clean yourself during this bath to raise your positive vibration. You can use vanilla candles for the same result.

- Sip the "I Love Me a Latte" (page 49) in the bath to enchant the self-love vibes of the waters.

CHAKRA ME BACK TO LIFE

A coffee scrub to help you get back into alignment

Chakras are the spiritual energy centers within our bodies that help regulate the flow of energy. There are seven main chakras, from the soles of our feet to the very top of our head. When these chakras are all open, they work in perfect harmony, creating balance and spiritual alignment. However, more often than not, one or more of our chakras become blocked, throwing our entire spiritual system out of whack. Fortunately, you can get yourself back in alignment with a little meditation, self-care, and some coffee.

---

a bowl

a spoon

½ cup coffee grounds (*either fresh or leftover coffee grounds*)

½ cup white granulated sugar

¼ cup melted coconut oil

an airtight container

a bathtub or shower

MEDICAL NOTE: Before you put this scrub on your body, please do a quick patch test to make sure you don't have a reaction to the scrub, especially if you have sensitive skin.

THE RITUAL

STEP 1: In your bowl, with a spoon, mix your coffee grounds, sugar, and coconut oil together until totally combined.

STEP 2: Take your mixture and place it into the airtight container.

STEP 3: When you're ready to use your scrub, undress completely. Close your eyes and take a deep belly breath in and out.

STEP 4: Take a small amount of your scrub on the tips of your finger and place it on the top of both of your feet. This area is ruled by the root chakra. Picture in your mind's eye a red glow around your feet. Gently rub in a circular motion on your skin. As you do this, picture that light getting bigger and brighter, opening up.

STEP 5: Take a small amount of scrub on the tips of your finger and place it on the area just below your navel. This area is ruled by the sacral chakra. Picture in your mind's eye an orange glow around that area. Gently rub in a circular motion on your skin. As you do this, picture that light getting bigger and brighter, opening up.

STEP 6: Take a small amount of scrub and place it on the base of your rib cage. This area is ruled by the solar plexus chakra. Picture in your mind's eye a yellow glow around that area. Gently rub in a circular motion on your skin. As you do this, picture that light getting bigger and brighter, opening up.

STEP 7: Take a small amount of scrub and place it on the center of your chest. This area is ruled by the heart chakra. Picture in your mind's eye a green glow around that area. Gently rub in a circular motion on your skin. As you do this, picture that light getting bigger and brighter, opening up.

STEP 8: Take a small amount of scrub and place it on the center of your neck. This area is ruled by the throat chakra. Picture in your mind's eye a blue glow around that area. Gently rub in a circular motion on your skin. As you do this, picture that light getting bigger and brighter, opening up.

STEP 9: Take a small amount of scrub and place it in the area between your eyebrows. This area is ruled by third-eye chakra. Picture in your mind's eye an indigo glow around that area. Gently rub in a circular motion on your skin. As you do this, picture that light getting bigger and brighter, opening up.

STEP 10: Take a small amount of scrub and place it on the top part of your head, without it getting in your hair. This area is ruled by the crown chakra. Picture in your mind's eye a white glow around that area. Gently rub in a circular motion on your skin. As you do this, picture that light getting bigger and brighter, opening up.

STEP 11: When you are finished, take in another deep belly breath. As you do this, imagine your chakras in their colors, all bright, bold, and clear. Imagine the energy that is in your body flowing easily between all seven of them. Breathe out.

STEP 12: Hop in the shower or bath and wash the scrub away. As you do this, visualize yourself cleaning all the dirt and grime from your chakras, completely unblocking them. Keep the rest of your scrub in the container to use again when you feel blocked.

FOR A DASH OF MAGIC...

Wash the scrub off in the "Cleanse Me in Coffee" bath on page 116 for an extra cleansing boost.

- If you don't want to do a full scrub, you can also put a small amount on the chakra that you think is blocked. For example, if you're going through a major creative block, put some of the scrub on your sacral chakra.

- Brew "Red Eye for the Third Eye" on page 51 and sip it during or after your scrub ritual to help open your third eye.

- For best results, do this during a full moon for maximum healing.

ONE LAST CUP
Celebrating a soul that is no longer with us

Mexico has an annual holiday called Día de Muertos, "Day of the Dead," at the beginning of November, celebrating and remembering loved ones who have passed on from this world, creating altars and placing the things they enjoyed in life on those altars, often including coffee. In this ritual, we will be doing something similar, where you have one more cup of coffee with the person you love.

---

a table

a photo of your loved one

one yellow candle

items that your loved one enjoyed *(optional)*

2 cups coffee

THE RITUAL

STEP 1: Pick your altar location. Your altar can be anywhere you like. It can be at your kitchen table, it can be in a corner of your home, or it can even be a part of your coffee bar altar. It just needs to be on a table or a flat surface.

STEP 2: Once you pick your altar location, set up your altar. You can keep it simple by just placing a photo of your loved one and the candle there or you can add things that your loved one enjoyed in life. Whatever feels right to you and what you think they would enjoy will be perfect. If you have a letter that you wrote to them, place it at the altar.

STEP 3: Make the coffee for two people, one cup for them and one for you. Make their favorite cup of coffee using the brands, flavors, and methods that they liked. Be mindful and present as you craft these drinks, like you're making it just for them. If your loved one enjoyed a certain coffee shop, pick up their drink there.

STEP 4: When you are finished, place their coffee in front of the altar.

STEP 5: Light the yellow candle. This acts as a guiding light to welcome the spirit to the altar.

STEP 6: Sit next to or in front of the altar and sip your coffee. If you wish, you can talk out loud to your loved one, you can play them some music, or sit quietly and enjoy the coffee. Whatever feels right to you.

STEP 7: When you're ready, put your coffee cup down and say: "Thank you for having coffee with me. Have safe passage back to the spirit world. I love you," and blow out the candle.

STEP 8: You can either leave their coffee on the table, drink it yourself, or give it to another loved one. If no one drinks it, pour it back into the earth.

FOR A DASH OF MAGIC...

You can also reverse this and make it a banishing ritual. See "Get the Hex Out" on page 183.

IT'S IN THE BAG
A manifestation ritual

Manifestation is a conscious effort to make our thoughts and desires into tangible realities. Manifestation rituals can take many forms, from writing our desires down on paper to visualizations and practicing gratitude. In fact, almost every spell, ritual, and potion in this book is a form of manifestation because it is an action you're taking in the hope of bringing what you want to reality, whether it's a certain outcome or a feeling. Here, we have a quick ritual to help you boost the energy of your manifestation and make what you desire come a little faster. Remember, it's in the bag.

a little sachet bag

½ cup dark roast coffee beans *(deep meditation, accuracy, introspection, and foresight)*

1 tablespoon dried ground ginger or 1 piece of whole dried ginger *(confidence, clarity, quick manifestation, inner power, abundance, balance, success)*

1 tablespoon dried cayenne pepper flakes *(removes obstacles, speeds things up, road opening, motivation, cleansing, protection, courage)*

2 teaspoons granulated sugar *(attraction, manifesting, multiplying)*

1 piece of moonstone *(guiding light, deep intuition, connecting to your higher purpose)*

1 piece of tiger's eye *(personal power, confidence, active manifestation)*

a small token that represents your manifestation

THE RITUAL

STEP 1: Take your sachet and fill it with your coffee beans, ginger, cayenne, sugar, crystals, and a small token that represents what you are hoping to manifest in your session. For example, if you are trying to manifest money, drop a few coins into your bag. If you're trying to manifest a house, place a mini figurine of a house in the bag. You can also add pictures.

STEP 2: Hold the bag in front of you and say: "All that I need is already within. However, a boost of intention and magic never hurts." Close the bag.

STEP 3: Get comfortable. Either sit in a comfortable chair or lie down. Place your bag in your hands or have it rest on your stomach or lap.

STEP 4: Close your eyes. Take a moment to get your breathing in rhythm. Take big belly breaths in and out. This is to help relax you and to calm any lingering anxieties you may be feeling.

STEP 5: When you're ready, visualize what you want the most. Picture yourself living like you already have that. For example, if you wish to manifest moving to a new city, visualize yourself living in that city. Picture what your apartment looks like, where you go grocery shopping, your commute, what you would do for fun. Don't think "I really want this," think "it's happening now."

STEP 6: As you visualize, hold on to your bag tightly, feeling the flow of energy move from the bag to your body.

STEP 7: When you finish your visualization and feel satisfied with your vision, say "Thank you, universe," and open your eyes. Continue with the rest of your day.

FOR A DASH OF MAGIC...

You can also drink this ritual by grinding the beans and adding a teaspoon of ginger to the grounds. Then, stir in a pinch of cayenne and a teaspoon of sugar. Sip this while doing your ritual.

You can easily swap out different herbs and crystals to best match your intentions. For example, if you wish to manifest love in your life, add rose quartz and put in dried rose petals. If you're manifesting money, add a piece of pyrite and allspice to the mix. If you're looking to manifest happiness, use a yellow sachet.

Combine this ritual with the "Just Like Magic" spell on page 154 by casting the spell first and sipping the coffee as you do the ritual.

You can also combine these rituals with other manifesting practices like the 33 x 3 manifestation where you write what you desire (for example, writing "I'm so happy I got the big promotion at work") thirty-three times in a row for three days in a row. Keep your sachet on your lap as you write.

Sleep with this sachet under your pillow at night to manifest while you sleep.

COFFEE MAGIC *for the* MODERN WITCH

A MOMENT TO GET GROUNDED
A coffee Zen garden to chill out

While you most likely can't put a full altar at your desk at work without getting a few stares, you can make a Zen garden with a coffee twist. Not only can it help relieve your stress when work gets you down, but it can also act as a mini altar in plain sight.

---

a shallow glass bowl

1 cup fresh coffee grounds

crystals (*any kind of crystals that you desire, though keep them on the smaller side so you can move them around with your rake easily*)

other small trinkets (*optional*)

a mini rake (*you can also make your own mini rake out of coffee stirrers*)

THE RITUAL

STEP 1: Take your glass bowl and pour in your coffee grounds. Swirl the grounds around three times counterclockwise. This is to banish any negative energy, only leaving good vibes.

STEP 2: Add in your crystals. You can put them in any order you desire and you can use as many crystals as you want, as long you don't fill the bowl full of them! You can also add other things that you've found to your garden, such as small rocks or sea glass, mini figurines, charms, or whatever fits your aesthetic. Don't be afraid to play around with this.

STEP 3: Take your mini rake and draw a circle in the grounds three times, clockwise. This brings positive energy into the bowl.

STEP 4: Enjoy it! Use this to help ground yourself when you're feeling too stressed out. From drawing shapes, patterns, and sigils to clear your mind and get away from a stressful situation, to just smelling the coffee for a boost of energy, this is your little space to get calm again.

FOR A DASH OF MAGIC...

✳ Use your rake to write sigils in the coffee "sands" as a tiny spell or mantra to get you through the day. You can also use this to test out sigils (see "Sigil Magic" on page 144 for more details).

✳ You can use your mini Zen garden as a place to do a rune reading. A rune reading or rune casting is a fortune-telling method that uses stones with the ancient Germanic alphabet Elder Futhark on each stone. These stones can tell you about your past, present, and future, similar to a tarot card reading. Take a bag of runes and pour them into your garden. Use your rake to swirl the sands and stones around and pull your stones at random.

✳ Pick out your crystals based on what energy you need. For example, if you're stressed out because of money, put green aventurine in your garden.

✳ To keep the magic fresh, replace the grounds with new ones every month. Or pick a glass bowl with a lid to keep the coffee fresh when not in use.

LET ME SPELL IT OUT FOR YOU
A coffee ink for writing rituals

Most writers will tell you coffee fuels them to finish their work, meet their deadlines, and even fire up their creative spark. As I write this, I'm currently drinking my fourth cup of the day. However, coffee isn't just creative fuel for our bodies, we can also put the magical benefits of coffee directly on the page. Coffee ink is perfect for writing spells, taking notes, and enchanting important words. For this ritual, we'll be creating coffee ink to help manifest our desires for the day.

---

1 teaspoon instant coffee

a glass jar

2 tablespoons hot water

a spoon

paper (*preferably watercolor paper*)

a paintbrush or dip pen

THE RITUAL

STEP 1: Pour your instant coffee into your jar. Then pour in your hot water and stir clockwise with a spoon. Instant coffee is the best way to make coffee ink as it creates a thicker liquid and a darker color than using regular coffee. If you want to create more ink, add in more instant coffee and hot water.

STEP 2: Get your writing area ready; you can do this anywhere from your desk to your kitchen table, just as long as you have a solid place to put your paper and ink on. I recommend watercolor paper as the ink will have a similar texture to watercolor paint, and the paper will catch the color nicely. However, you are free to use whatever paper you like, just make sure it's thick enough that the ink won't bleed through.

STEP 3: For this ritual, we're going to write a simple affirmation to get us started. When you get used to coffee ink, you can get more creative with what you want to do with the ink. On your paper, take your paintbrush or dip pen and write: "I stir up good vibes."

STEP 4: Write this several times until you fill up your paper.

STEP 5: Wait for your ink to dry. When you're finished, you can place it by your altar, hang it up, or burn it. The choice is yours. If you have leftover coffee ink, put a lid on the jar and save it for next time.

FOR A DASH OF MAGIC...

* This is a great way to write spells and create sigils (see "Sigil Magic" on page 144), especially if you want the magical benefits of coffee and don't want to use ink.

* Use coffee ink to practice psychography, the divination method of using automatic writing to predict the future and understand your subconscious mind. Make your coffee ink, meditate for a few moments, then start writing. Don't even look at what you're writing down until the end, just keep writing whatever comes to you first without thinking or

overanalyzing it. Read over what you wrote. You can also do this with painting.

* Coffee ink is great for journaling as constantly dipping your pen into the ink allows you to slow down and really analyze your thoughts and ideas. Use coffee ink when writing down divination reading observations as they can help you think things through.

* Use coffee ink for creative art projects that infuse magic and art together.

* Add coffee ink writing to your "Magic Morning Witch-ual" (see page 96).

* Coffee ink can also be a dye, so use it to stain the pages of your grimoire for an old-school witchy look or dye your tarot bag to infuse the magic of the coffee into your cards.

A CUP FULL OF LIGHT
A coffee candle-making ritual

Who doesn't love the smell of coffee? Obviously, you must love it, or you wouldn't have picked up this book! Sometimes we want the smell of coffee or the magical properties that coffee provides without having to make (and drink) the whole pot. Fortunately, you can get that aromatic coffee shop smell—by lighting a candle. While making your very own candle seems like an intimidating task, it's not as hard as you may think. And, by making your own candle, you are creating a tool that is completely infused with your energy. Each time you light your candle, you'll be sparking up your intent and energy into the room. How magical!

WITCHES' SAFETY TIP: Throughout this ritual, we will be working with wax and boiling water, which can be a potential fire hazard. Please remember to practice good fire safety and be careful near an open flame and hot water.

---

1 coffee mug or mason jar

12 ounces plain, unscented soy candle wax *(recycled or new, you can order candle wax online or at a craft store)*

a heat-safe container *(tempered glass or aluminum)*

1 candle wick

a candle glue dot or a hot glue gun

a pair of chopsticks or wooden sticks

a saucepan

1 cup water

1 tablespoon dark roast coffee grounds *(fresh or used)*
candy-making thermometer
strainer
oven mitts

———— ❊ ————

THE RITUAL

STEP 1: Choose your candleholder. Consider an old mug that you've stopped using but still love the look of, or you can use a mason jar. Whatever fits your vibe (or whatever you have on hand) will be fine.

STEP 2: Use your candleholder to measure your candle wax. 12 ounces of wax should be great for an 8- or 10-ounce mug, but make sure to measure it to see if you need a little more (or a little less). Ideally, you should have enough wax to fill your candleholder one and a half times. Always make extra: it's better to have too much wax and save some for later than having to do the whole process again to make more wax.

STEP 3: When you have measured your wax, place the wax in a heat-safe container like a tempered-glass measuring cup (one that you only use for candle making) or an aluminum can.

STEP 4: Take your wick and place your candle glue dot on your wick. You can also use a glue gun, but be careful not to burn the candle to the very bottom as the clue is flammable. Affix the wick to the center of the bottom of your candleholder and let it dry for about an hour. Wrap the excess amount of wick around one of the chopsticks and place it at the opening of your cup, horizontally. This will hold your wick upright when it's time to pour the wax.

STEP 5: Set your stove to low-medium heat and add the cup of water to the saucepan. Wait for the water to heat up but don't let it boil.

STEP 6: Place your heat-safe container filled with wax into your saucepan. Make sure that the water reaches halfway up the outside of the container, does not touch the rim, and that the container doesn't touch the sides of the saucepan.

STEP 7: Wait for the wax to melt. Do not leave the wax unattended as it could be a potential fire hazard.

STEP 8: When the wax has melted, take your tablespoon of coffee grounds, pour it into the wax, and stir with your other chopstick or wooden stick. Fresh dark roast coffee is best for a strong scent. However, you can also work with used coffee grounds; just make sure you have dried them first.

STEP 9: Allow the wax to heat for a couple more minutes to make sure to infuse the coffee's scent and color into the mix.

STEP 10: Turn off the stove and allow your container to cool a little, but don't let it get under 100°F, or the wax will start to solidify. Use your candy-making thermometer to keep an eye on it.

STEP 11: Place your strainer over your candleholder; this will get rid of the remaining grounds and act as a funnel for your candle wax.

STEP 12: When your container is cool enough, slip on your oven mitts and take your container out of the water, pouring the wax into the strainer, which will go directly into the candleholder. Pour in about three-quarters of the wax.

STEP 13: Let the wax cool completely at room temperature. This can take from a few hours to a day. When the wax is cool, there may be a small well at the center of the handle. This is normal. Just reheat the quarter of wax that you saved earlier and pour it into the candle. This will fill the rest of the candle and cover up any wells or gaps in it.

STEP 14: Allow the wax to harden again. When it's solid, unravel your wick from the chopstick and trim the wick to ⅛ inch long above the candle.

STEP 15: Light your candle and feel the magic.

FOR A DASH OF MAGIC...

- If you wish to impart more magical intent to the candle, add in some scent extracts to the wax when you put in your coffee grounds. If you wish to use this candle for luck and prosperity spells and rituals, add in a few drops of peppermint extract. If you wish to make this a love spell, add a few drops of vanilla extract. If you wish to make this a study candle, add in some maple extract. You can also use coffee grounds that are already infused with flavor, like cinnamon-infused coffee or chocolate-raspberry coffee.

- Once your wax has hardened, carve in a sigil that represents your intent for this candle. For example, if you wish to use this candle for money spells or abundance rituals, carve in a money sigil (see "Sigil Magic" on page 144).

- Keep this candle at your coffee bar altar for a shot of magic.

- Keep at your altar during the "One Last Cup" ritual on page 122.

LATE NIGHT AU LAIT
A good-night ritual

Part of my nightly ritual is that I always drink a cup of coffee before bed. This always gets a side-eye from people: "Why would you drink caffeine right before bed? Won't that keep you up?" However, I've never had a problem sleeping after drinking coffee, easily falling asleep after one or even two cups. For me, it's the ritual of having a warm cup of coffee, allowing myself to relax and unwind from the day, and mentally preparing for the next. This is meant to help you set up a calming nightly ritual of making a café au lait, a drink that can bring comfort, peace, and sleep. *Fais de beaux rêves!*

½ cup decaf coffee

½ cup milk *(any kind)*

a mug

a spoon

a snack *(optional)*

your grimoire *(optional)*

a tarot deck *(optional)*

amethyst crystal *(for sleep, relaxation, and smoothing of the mind and spirit)*

THE RITUAL

STEP 1: Before you start, please turn off or silence all technology. Doom-scrolling before bed isn't the best way to get some decent sleep.

STEP 2: Put on your pajamas and start some of the nightly rituals you already have (taking a shower, doing your skin-care routine, packing your lunch for work the next day, etc.).

STEP 3: Brew your coffee. I recommend decaf coffee as it has less caffeine, so it won't keep you up. However, keep in mind that café au lait is typically made with strong coffee, so this will taste a little weaker. If caffeine before bed doesn't bother you, feel free to use strong coffee.

STEP 4: While your coffee is brewing, steam your milk. You can do this by either heating your milk in a saucepan and whisking it until it's slightly foamy, or microwaving your milk and using a handheld frother or French press to froth it. As you steam your milk, think of all the good dreams you wish to have, or how a good night's sleep is going to feel after a long day.

STEP 5: Add your coffee to your mug. Take your spoon and stir your drink three times counterclockwise to banish any negative energy that may prevent you from sleeping peacefully.

STEP 6: Add in your steamed milk. Take the drink into your bedroom with you. If you want a snack, grab it now.

STEP 7: Get into bed. While sitting up, close your eyes and take a deep belly breath in and out a few times to help you relax and get grounded.

STEP 8: When you're ready, sip your drink. While you drink, you can write in your journal or grimoire, eat your snack, do a reflective tarot card reading, or hold your amethyst crystal and meditate. Whatever feels more relaxing to you.

STEP 9: Once you get to the last sip of your café au lait, say "Good night and sweet dreams," and take that last sip.

STEP 10: Finish the rest of your nightly rituals if you have any and go to sleep.

FOR A DASH OF MAGIC...

* Add a little lavender syrup to your drink or add some dried lavender on top of your drink as lavender is associated with peace, calm, and sleep.

* Perform the "Nightmare Be Gone" spell (page 150) before this ritual to prevent nightmares.

* For snack ideas, eat a blueberry scone for calming and good cheer. Nibble on a honey-butter croissant to replenish your energy.

Chapter 4

SPELLIN' THE BEANS
Coffee Spells for Every Occasion

○ ☽ ✸ ☾ ○

A spell, at its core, is a series of words that are said with magical intent to be manifested into energy and action. So, while this can be a bunch of rhyming words or fake Latin, it can also be done in simple ways that you've probably already seen performed over a hundred times in your life. You've probably even performed a spell without realizing it. Singing the lyrics to a song that you're deeply connected to? That's a spell. Writing in your journal about the hopes you have for the future? That's a spell. Words have power, and what we say, good or bad, can lead to some serious manifestation. Remember, "thoughts become reality," so it's important to focus on the good thoughts, the hopeful thoughts, rather than the ones that are infused with negativity, anxiety, and self-doubt.

Also, don't worry about wording your spells like a legal contract or putting in extra effort to make them sound "witchy" enough. This isn't a test. To make a spell work, truly work, you have to put your energy and feeling into it. If you truly believe that you're going to get a certain outcome by the words you say, it'll come. Remember, the power of spells comes from within you. If you are alive, you are magic. Visualize the results and keep an open mind. You'll be fine.

A MODERN WITCH'S SPELL-CASTING TIPS

Remove the word "no" from your vocabulary: Have you ever said to yourself "I would not want X to happen" and then almost immediately, X happens. Like, "Good thing there's no delays on my way to work," and suddenly *everything* is delayed? If that has happened to you, you're not alone, and it's not because the universe hates you (I promise), but it's because the universe doesn't acknowledge any negative words or words of lack like "no," "not," "don't," and "never." Whenever the universe hears those words, it immediately skips over them. When you say, "I don't want to break up with my partner," the universe hears "I want to break up with my partner." If you're casting a spell, saying "I'm not going to lose my job," you may be working against your best interest. Instead, say: "I'm successful in my career. I am thriving in my profession." This will get you closer to want you want.

Be clear: In that same vein, you always should be clear about your desired result. Being vague won't get you anywhere. So don't cast a spell saying "I want to be in a relationship" when you really want to be with your soulmate. Not all relationships are romantic, and not all relationships are healthy and positive. Instead, cast a spell saying, "I'm in a healthy, positive, romantic relationship with the person who is my soulmate." Nice and clear. Notice I'm speaking in the present tense. That's because "I want" or "I need" are also statements of lack. Saying "I want a new car" in a spell is telling the universe that you don't have something, and with no action being taken, the universe is less likely to give it to you. However, if you cast a spell saying "My new car is working perfectly and I'm so happy with it," you are putting it in your life, so the universe is more likely to make it happen. Remember, if you aren't sure about what you want, hold off on casting a spell. It won't work unless you have the conviction and drive to back it up.

Believe in your own magic: In this life, the person you have to believe in the most is yourself. To trust that you have the power to make the best choices for you, to improve your life for the better, and serve your highest good. It can be hard for a lot of people; it's hard for me. Believing in ourselves and trusting ourselves can be a difficult task, especially when we are overly self-critical and lack confidence. However, for magic to work, we need to believe it is within us. If you cast a spell thinking "I'm hopeless at this, I'll just screw up," chances are your spell won't work. You need to be in a positive emotional and mental headspace to get positive results. Believe in your own power and you will be unstoppable.

Connect words with actions: Words have power; however, if you want that power to manifest into something tangible, you're going to have to put in the work to make it happen. Whether it's waving a wand, making a drink, lighting a candle, drawing a picture, or taking care of a plant, you have to take some action in order for a spell to activate. This is to charge up your spell with your unique energy, giving it life. This is also showing the universe that you are willing to make an effort to make your spell come true. Also, it's easier to believe in your spell if you're performing an action with it. Even if you're just drinking a cup of coffee.

Always give yourself an out: If you're worried about a spell completely blowing up in your face, both literally and metaphorically, always end your spell with "for my highest good," which is basically a magical loophole for "if this isn't right for me, don't give it to me." We often don't know what fate has planned for us until it happens. Something that we thought we want may not be something that we want later. For example, say you are looking into moving to a new place. You have your eye on your "dream" apartment and cast a spell to get it. However, the apartment eventually goes to someone else. While you're crushed, you continue to go on your search and eventually find a place that you love and can afford. It's not what you wanted originally, but it turns out to be perfect for you. You later find out through reviews that your "dream" apartment actually had a lot of issues, and the landlord is a pain to deal with. You get what was best for your highest good, not what you think is good.

ALL IN THE TIMING...

Timing is everything, so when you start casting your spells, be mindful about when you're casting them, as certain days of the weeks, or the phase of the moon, may help your spell flourish. This isn't to say you should put your spell on hold until the full moon (especially if it's a really important spell), but be mindful that when you choose to cast affects your results.

Here are some things to look out for.

THE MOON IS ON YOUR SIDE

The moon is a powerful force that can bring an extra oomph of power to all aspects of your craft. Traditionally, most witches like to perform spells under the light of the full moon for the drama. However, all parts of the lunar cycle hold unique magical energy that can aid you when working on a particular spell.

- ⚝ **New Moon:** Cleansing spells, setting intentions, divination, and starting new things. This is a time for new beginnings.

- ⚝ **Waxing Crescent:** Manifesting, attraction, prosperity, inspiration, energy, health, and luck spells.

- ⚝ **First Quarter:** Strength, building momentum, fertility spells, and transformation spells. This is a time for growth and taking action. Now is the time to make a serious effort.

- ⚝ **Waxing Gibbous:** Growth and protection spells, manifesting hopes and dreams. This is a great time to take a step back to see what part of your plan needs a little fine-tuning.

- ⚝ **Full Moon:** Charging, healing spells, and practicing gratitude. This is a period of clarity as you see what is hidden. Also, a great time for making changes and celebrating success.

- ⚝ **Waning Gibbous:** Cleansing and banishment. Reflecting on lessons we have learned.

- ⚝ **Last Quarter:** Unbinding spells, introspection, forgiveness, sharing with others. Getting rid of what no longer is working for you.

- ⚝ **Waning Crescent:** Scrying, meditation, self-care, and rest. Preparing for the next cycle of life.

A MAGICAL WEEK

You can also schedule your spells just by looking at your calendar. Each day of the week is associated with a certain planet that rules over that day, giving it certain influence and power that work better for different kinds of spells.

* ✵ **Monday:** Associated with the moon; good for fertility spells, divination, increasing dreams, and spirituality.

* ✵ **Tuesday:** Associated with Mars; good for spells associated with conquering obstacles, dealing with conflict, taking action, increasing energy, and gaining independence.

* ✵ **Wednesday:** Associated with Mercury; good for creativity spells, communication spells, job spells, and career spells.

* ✵ **Thursday:** Associated with Jupiter; good for money spells, business spells, legal matters.

* ✵ **Friday:** Associated with Venus; good for love spells, relationship spells, and sex spells.

* ✵ **Saturday:** Associated with Saturn; good for protection spells, overcoming habits, banishment spells, binding spells, and meditation.

* ✵ **Sunday:** Associated with the sun; good for success spells, abundance spells, strength, happiness spells, and healing spells.

SIGIL MAGIC

If you're not a writer or particularly good with words, no worries! Spells don't have to be word based. You can also cast spells using art and symbols, known as "sigil magic." Sigil magic is a type of spell that uses drawing and symbols that are created and charged with magical meaning. Think of this as your magical signature that you put at the end of your ritual, brew, or other spell for a magical boost.

CREATING A SIGIL

Any type of drawing can be a sigil if you put your intent into it when you create it, from doodles to unique codes that you made up with your besties. However, if you're not sure where to start, here's a common way to create sigils based on your intent to create a one-of-a-kind drawing you can use to work your magic.

STEP 1: Think about the sigil you'd like to create; what is its purpose? What do you want it to manifest for you? For this example, let's say you are looking for love, so you'll need a love sigil.

STEP 2: Think of the word that closely resembles what you want. If you are casting a protection sigil, you may want to use words like "safe" or "shield." For abundance, you may want to use the word "money" or "prosperity." You can also use full sentences like "Make me rich" or "Everything I need is within me." For our love sigil, let's keep it simple and use "love."

STEP 3: Write out your word. Then remove the vowels. So, for "love" we would take out the *o* and *e*, leaving this:

L V

Those are the shapes that you have to work with.

STEP 4: Play around with the *L* and the *V* until you get a design that you like. You can experiment with this as much as you want: uppercase, lowercase, cursive, print; you can even use a different language. Just make sure they are in the drawing in some way. Here is my sigil for love. Feel free to use it.

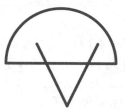

Remember, this is supposed to be fun and allow you to express your creative magic. So don't think too hard about what the sigil looks like. It doesn't have to be "perfect"; in fact, many sigils are created just to be destroyed (by drinking, eating, burning, tearing up, etc.), so you can always draw a different one next time. Just draw something that you really love that means something to you. And remember, you can always change it.

Now that we understand spell casting in all of its forms, let's make some magic!

DRAW ME A SPELL
Sigil latte art!

As I mentioned in the chapter introduction, sigils can be drawn anywhere, from the outside of your cup to the bottom of your glass. However, if you really want to get creative with your spell casting, make it into latte art! Latte art is a design on top of drinks like lattes, cappuccinos, and other milk-foam beverages. This is done by either pouring the milk foam over the espresso in your latte in a certain way to create a pattern or by drawing a particular pattern within the foam to create some magic.

---

1 shot espresso

wide-mouth shallow cup

½ cup milk *(any but recommend whole milk, soy milk, and oat milk for texture and thickness)*

stainless steel milk pitcher

latte pen or toothpick

stencils *(optional)*

cocoa, cinnamon, or nutmeg powder *(optional, for stencil)*

chocolate or caramel syrup *(optional)*

HOW TO CONJURE

STEP 1: Make your espresso in your preferred way and pour it into your cup. You can also do latte art with regular coffee (preferably

2–3 ounces of coffee) but keep in mind it won't be as strong or cut through the milk as well as when using espresso.

STEP 2: Heat up your milk until it's steaming. Then froth the milk with your preferred method (milk frother, French press, pour into a jar and shake, etc.). Pour it into the milk pitcher.

STEP 3: Swirl your milk in your pitcher clockwise three times to get all the bubbles out of the pitcher. If there are still some bubbles, gently tap the pitcher on the counter three times.

STEP 4: Hold your cup at an angle and pour in your milk from a high distance so the milk dives beneath the surface of the espresso. Do this slowly.

STEP 5: When the cup is half full, lower the pitcher a little and increase the speed of your pour while tilting your cup straight up again. Move the pitcher in a clockwise motion. Pour until your cup is almost full.

STEP 6: When the white microfoam starts to appear, you can begin your design. You can make a design in a variety of ways. You can pour a dot in the center and use your latte pen or toothpicks to make the design. You can dip your latte pen/toothpick in your syrup and draw out your sigil or words. You can also use stencils to make your design by putting the stencil over the foam and tracing it with the pen or putting cinnamon or cocoa dust on top. Do what feels right to you.

STEP 7: As you design, visualize what you want to manifest with this sigil. If this is an abundance spell, visualize having all the money you need. If you're creating a sign for success, visualize yourself achieving your ambition as you design.

COFFEE MAGIC *for the* **MODERN WITCH**

STEP 8: When you're finished, sip your drink and feel those vibes as you drink. Remember, it'll take you a few tries to get the hang of it, so don't be discouraged if you don't have Instagrammable latte art on your first try. As long as you add in your intent, your sigil spell will work. No matter how it looks.

FOR A DASH OF MAGIC...

☀ Dip your latte pen/toothpick into chocolate syrup if you're creating prosperity spells, love spells, friendship spells, or need some grounding. Use caramel syrup if you're looking to create spells for soothing and comfort, transformation spells, or adding a boost of positivity.

☀ You can also dip your latte pen/toothpick into any of the syrups you created in Chapter Two to make your art in the latte foam, which will infuse the properties of that syrup into your sigil.

☀ Use cinnamon powder on your stencil for luck, success, energy, happiness, creativity, money, healing, protection, and love sigil spells.

☀ Use nutmeg powder in your stencil for luck, travel, attraction, intuition, justice, prosperity, and lust sigils and spells.

NIGHTMARE BE GONE

A nightmare removal spell to promote good dreams

Coffee isn't known for helping us sleep—in fact, it's famous for keeping us up all night. However, if you have nightmares plaguing your sleep or preventing you from resting peacefully, coffee can be an elixir to banish those bad dreams with a little help from some magic beans.

---

a lavender candle with matches *(calming, peace, relaxation)*
a blue pouch
1 cup whole coffee beans *(banishing nightmares, grounding, protection)*
3 pieces of star anise *(wards off nightmares)*

HOW TO CONJURE

STEP 1: Do your regular bedtime routine as usual. Sit on your bed and light your lavender candle. Take a moment to breathe in the scent of the lavender and get your mind to settle down after a long day.

STEP 2: When you're ready, take out your blue pouch and place your coffee beans inside. As you pour them in, say: "With these beans, I'll cleanse my dreams and be at peace."

STEP 3: Add in your 3 pieces of star anise, while saying: "Star anise, be my guide. Keep my dreams peaceful and bright."

STEP 4: Hold the bag in front of you and say, three times: "With this pouch, I banish nightmares from my sleep. I will find sweeter dreams again."

STEP 5: Put your pouch under your pillow. Before blowing out your candle, say, "For my highest good," to complete the spell.

STEP 6: Go to sleep and have pleasant dreams.

FOR A DASH OF MAGIC...

- Sip some decaf coffee with vanilla syrup to sweeten your dreams.
- Write down all the dreams you want to have on a small piece of paper. Fold it up and place it in your pouch.
- Before going to bed, meditate with your nightmare-removal pouch to help you get in a good mindset before sleep.
- Perform the "Late Night au Lait" ritual on page 136 to help you relax and get ready for sleep.

LET'S SPEED THINGS ALONG
A spell booster to make things happen

In a world of instant gratification, beginning witches and spell casters may feel a little frustrated when the spells that they cast don't automatically manifest the moment they cast them. When getting into the craft, the first and most important lesson that one must learn is the art of patience.

Having said that, sometimes we could use a boost. If you're casting a spell that needs to work sooner rather than later, need to strengthen your spell, or perk up a reoccurring spell, coffee can be an easy hack to move things along. Here is how to use coffee grounds to make your spells work twice as fast.

———————— �֍ ————————

an airtight container
1 cup dark roast coffee grounds (*meditation, accuracy*)
1 teaspoon instant espresso powder (*speed, quickness, energy*)
an altar with a spell already in place

———————— ✖ ————————

HOW TO CONJURE

STEP 1: In an airtight container, mix the coffee grounds and the espresso powder together. Keep the container in a safe place.

STEP 2: When you need it, take out the container and sprinkle some of the coffee mix on your altar with your left hand after you've cast your spell. Make sure that the grounds form a complete circle. As you sprinkle, say: "To speed things along, have a boost of coffee and let's get moving. For my highest good."

STEP 3: Keep the grounds where they are and go about your day. Replace with fresh grounds when needed until things begin to move along.

FOR A DASH OF MAGIC...

* If you don't want to leave coffee grounds at your altar, use a coffee-scented candle in your original spell to give it that extra energy boost. Or make your own candle using the "A Cup Full of Light" ritual on page 132.

* Add a pinch of ground cinnamon to your mixture for success, energy, and protection.

* Cast a coffee circle around your bathtub during the "Cleanse Me in Coffee" ritual on page 116 to give you your energy back more quickly.

* Cast a coffee circle around your manifestation bag during the "It's in the Bag" ritual on page 124 to help you manifest faster.

* Cast a coffee circle when performing the "May Your Cup Runneth Over" spell on page 176 to help you manifest those good vibes a little more speedily.

JUST LIKE MAGIC
A spell for getting what you want

Look, we can all use a little more abundance in our lives. Whether you need a little more cash to get you through or you're looking to improve your life with happiness and good vibes, it all starts with a fresh cup of coffee. This sweet and spicy coffee spell can help attract the abundance that you've been craving.

---

a saucepan

10 ounces medium roast coffee (*luck, positivity, happiness*)

10 ounces water

1 cinnamon stick (*luck, success, money, happiness, creativity*)

4 whole cloves (*protection, banishing negativity, money*)

3 teaspoons sugar (*attraction, love, manifesting*)

a coffee cup

HOW TO CONJURE

STEP 1: In a small saucepan, combine the coffee grounds, water, cinnamon stick, and cloves, and bring to a boil.

STEP 2: Remove from the heat and let the coffee stand for six minutes. Then, strain the cinnamon and cloves from the liquid.

STEP 3: Think about what you wish to attract right now. Love? Money? Success? Positive feelings? Come up with three things.

They could be love, friendship, and security. Or money, success, and recognition. Whatever you desire.

STEP 4: Take your sugar and pour it into the saucepan and stir three times, clockwise. As you stir, say: "With this sugar, I attract"—and say the first thing you wish to attract into your life. Continue this for the second and third thing you wish to attract into your life until the sugar dissolves.

STEP 5: Pour your coffee into your cup. Take a moment to ground yourself, visualizing yourself having everything you wish to attract. Sip and enjoy.

FOR A DASH OF MAGIC...

✳ Add some vanilla whipped cream on top for an extra boost of luck and wealth.

✳ Don't want to get too fancy? Make regular coffee and stir your brew with a cinnamon stick to give you some extra luck with every sip.

✳ If you want to speed this abundance along, add a tablespoon of espresso powder to your brew to give it a boost.

✳ Drink this before performing the "Nightmare Be Gone" spell (page 150) to help attract a good-night spell and kinder dreams.

FRIENDSHIP IS MAGIC
A spell for a stronger relationship

Sometimes all you need to seal the deal is a good cup of coffee, whether you're going on a first date with someone special, making new friends at your favorite café, or celebrating the start of a beautiful business partnership. If you're looking to make your relationships even stronger, here's a spell that brings those bonds closer together and brews the beginning of a beautiful friendship. While it says "friendship" in the title, you can also use this for business and/or creative partnerships or romantic relationships.

ETHICAL NOTE: You can't forcibly bind someone to you or force someone to be your friend. This is simply to help things along, not change anyone's free will.

———— ※ ————

2 cups coffee (*preferably the "Let's Stick Together" drink from page 55, but use whatever coffee you like*)

2 mugs

rose quartz (*unconditional love and compassion*)

lapis lazuli (*communication and connection*)

amethyst (*serene and healthy friendships*)

1 tablespoon honey (*sweetening situations, binding, love, kindness, community, positivity, offering*)—*if not using the "Let's Stick Together" drink*

1 tablespoon molasses (*sweetening feelings, sticking to situations, business success, binding*)—*if not using the "Let's Stick Together" drink*

a spoon

caramel sauce (*friendship, transformation*)

———————— ·❊· ————————

HOW TO CONJURE

STEP 1: Brew your coffee and prepare it as you like.

STEP 2: Take two mugs and place them on your table. Take your crystals and place them around your cup with the amethyst on top, rose quartz to the left, and lapis lazuli to the right. They should form a crystal triangle around your cups.

STEP 3: Pour the honey and molasses into your two mugs. Make a sigil with it if you like.

STEP 4: Pour your coffee into the two cups. As you pour, say: "Sweet like honey and strong as molasses, when we stick together nothing can surpass us. For our highest good."

STEP 5: Stir. As you stir, pour all your good intention into the coffee and visualize the relationship you want to have with this person and how good it will be.

STEP 6: Pour your caramel sauce on top of the coffee in the sigil of friendship—whatever that may look like for you.

STEP 7: Serve your coffee. If the person is not with you, put their drink in front of a picture of them or a piece of paper with their name on it. This is a spiritual offering for that person.

STEP 8: Drink and enjoy.

FOR A DASH OF MAGIC...

※ For best results, make this on a Friday, as that is the day ruled by Venus and is associated with relationships.

※ For romantic relationships, brew the "You Mocha Me Crazy" potion on page 75 to seal the deal in your relationship.

※ For best results, do this during a new moon as a beautiful start to a new relationship.

※ You can also do this spell together over video chat for long-distance relationships (friendship or romantic) to strengthen your connection, even if you're miles away.

FROM THE GROUNDS UP

A gardening ritual for growth and protection

Coffee isn't just good for us, it's good for the earth as well. Many gardeners utilize coffee grounds in the garden, usually for composting. That's because coffee grounds are rich in nutrients, especially nitrogen, potassium, and phosphorus, which help plants grow. They are also great for keeping out pests, like insects. Whether you have a natural green thumb or are just trying to keep a plant alive, here's a green witch spell for growth and protection.

MEDICAL WARNING: Skip this spell if you have pets (especially dogs) because eating a large amount of coffee grounds from your garden can be harmful to their health.

---

plants that are already developed—blueberry bushes, roses, azaleas, hydrangeas, lilies, and African violets are preferred as they like a nitrogen-dense soil

a piece of paper

pen *(or coffee ink)*

a garden trowel

fresh or used coffee grounds

compost, shredded bark, or wood chips

water

HOW TO CONJURE

STEP 1: Pick a mature or developing plant to perform this spell on. Just like young humans, coffee is not good for seeds or new plants. Make sure this plant is close to your house if you're planting it outside. If your plant is inside, place it in front of the window and in a spot where you can see it every day.

STEP 2: Take your paper and tear off two very small pieces of it. On one piece of the paper, write something that you wish would grow right now. Maybe it's a love you have in a new relationship. Maybe it's the money in your bank account. Whatever you like.

STEP 3: On the second piece of paper, write out something that you wish to protect. It can be the name of a loved one; it can be yourself. It can even be your peace of mind. Anything!

STEP 4: Once you have everything written out, dig a small, shallow hole in the soil around your plant using your garden trowel. Place your two pieces of paper in the hole and cover it up.

STEP 5: Take your coffee grounds (if they are used, make sure they are fully dried) and lightly sprinkle a thin layer of coffee on the soil. As you sprinkle, say, three times: "I am safe and protected. I am nurtured and I'm growing. With every day, my dreams grow stronger."

STEP 6: When you're finished, cover your coffee grounds with compost, shredded bark, or wood chips.

STEP 7: Water your plant and take care of it. Every time you water it, you are helping your dreams grow.

FOR A DASH OF MAGIC...

- For best results, perform this spell on a new moon, as it the preferred time for new beginnings and new cycles.
- For extra magic, write out what you want to grow and protect in coffee ink. See "Let Me Spell It Out for You" on page 129.
- Choose your plant based on its magical properties. For example:
  - Blueberries are associated with optimism, beauty, memory, calm, protection, and intuition.
  - Roses are associated with love, glamour, divination, healing, compassion, protection, and calm.
  - Azaleas are associated with abundance, temperance, taking care of others, and passion but are also a death threat so be careful!
  - Hydrangeas are associated with love, lifting curses, and protection.
  - Lilies are associated with protection, purification, rebirth, emotions, strength, peace, and harmony.
  - African violets are associated with protection, enchanting magic, spirituality, and love.

NOTHING THAT COFFEE CAN'T SOLVE

For when all else has failed

Even the best witch finds herself in a bind every now and again, when we hit a certain problem and all other attempts, mundane and magical, have failed, and things start to feel a little desperate. When that happens, we may start to feel like we are failing in life. However, there is a saving grace you can do that may help you when everything else has failed. And no, we're not talking about making a deal with the devil (yet).

---

a small bowl

1/16 teaspoon ground cinnamon (*luck, success, happiness, creativity, healing, protection*)

1/16 teaspoon ground cayenne (*removing obstacles, opening road, breaking hexes, protecting, strength*)

1/16 teaspoon black pepper (*protection, cleansing, power, courage, creativity*)

1/16 teaspoon salt (*protection, purification*)

1 tablespoon white vinegar (*protection, banishing enemies*)

a large coffee filter

a trinket dish

piece of paper and pen (*or coffee ink*)

2 tablespoons coffee grounds

string

HOW TO CONJURE

STEP 1: In a small bowl, mix together the cinnamon, cayenne, black pepper, salt, and vinegar. Set aside.

STEP 2: At your altar (if you have one), place your coffee filter on top of the trinket dish. If you want to draw a sigil for whatever you think may help you with this problem, you can.

STEP 3: Take your paper and tear off a very small piece, just enough room to write a sentence on it. Write out the problem you are having. Really think about the true cause of the problem that has been plaguing you.

STEP 4: Fold the paper as small as you can make it. Then, dip your paper in the vinegar mixture that you made.

STEP 5: As you dip your paper in the mixture, say: "I leave my problem up to faith and banish this problem from my heart, mind, and soul. I need to find another way to go."

STEP 6: Place your paper on top of the coffee filter. Sprinkle the coffee grounds over the paper. As you do, say: "I bury my problem in the grounds in hopes of a solution or peace to sow. After all, there's nothing that coffee can't do."

STEP 7: When you're finished, take the coffee filter and twist to tie the top with your string. Leave it at your altar overnight. The next day, throw it away.

FOR A DASH OF MAGIC...

Add a pinch of cinnamon and cayenne on top of the coffee grounds for a magical boost to solve your problem more quickly.

* For best results, perform this spell on a Tuesday. Tuesday is ruled by Mars and good for spells associated with conquering obstacles and dealing with conflict.

* Perform the "Let's Speed Things Along" spell (page 152) after you do this spell to take care of this problem faster.

* Write your problem out in coffee ink (from the "Let Me Spell It Out for You" ritual on page 129) for an extra boost to speed up your solution.

* Light up a coffee candle (from the "A Cup Full of Light" ritual on page 132) and burn it while performing the spell—the coffee energy will help speed things along.

POUR ME ONE FOR THE ROAD
A spell for safe travel

There's nothing like a good cup of coffee before a road trip. It helps keep us going on long journeys, whether we're driving, riding, or flying (broomstick or otherwise). Here is a handy spell to conjure immediately before a trip to keep you protected on your adventure. This is also a great spell to keep a loved one safe on their travels.

---

2 teaspoons maple syrup (*travel, decision-making, dealing with change, protection, adaptability*)

travel mug

coffee (*prepared to your liking*)

¼ teaspoon ground nutmeg (*luck, travel, attraction*)

a spoon

HOW TO CONJURE

STEP 1: Add your maple syrup to your travel mug. As you pour, visualize the journey going smoothly, that you or your loved one get to the destination with no stress or anxiety. Say, either out loud or in your head: "My journey is smooth. I'm ready for anything that comes my way as it only adds to the adventure." If you're making this for someone, just insert their name.

STEP 2: Make your coffee the preferred way. As you make it, continue to think about the trip going smoothly. Go over your mental checklist of what you need to do and consider whether you've missed anything.

STEP 3: When your coffee is made, pour it into your travel mug. Add in your nutmeg. As you do, say: "With a dash of luck, everything will go my way. My journey will be a dream." Again, if you're making this for someone else, insert their name.

STEP 4: Stir your drink clockwise three times, and, as you stir, say: "My path is clear; my journey is set. Adventure awaits and I'm ready to greet whatever meets me." Or insert the person's name. Do this three times.

STEP 5: Sip and hit the road or give it to your loved one as they leave.

FOR A DASH OF MAGIC...

✳ While you can do this spell with any kind of coffee drink, a macchiato is recommended, as it has the magical properties of travel, protection, movement, and growth.

✳ You can also use this spell with "Basic Witches' Brew" (page 46) and "Changing Leaves, a Change in Me" (page 78), as they both have nutmeg and maple as key ingredients.

✳ Create a sigil on the bottom of your travel mug using maple syrup. If you're using a to-go cup, draw your sigil (see "Sigil Magic" on page 144) on it.

✳ Keep a crystal on hand to safeguard you as you travel. Here are a few travel-ready crystals:

   ✦ Malachite: Protects you from any danger and accidents. Also, helpful when dealing with change.

* Moonstone: Aids in travel anxiety and helps you open up to new beginnings and adventures.

* Smoky quartz: Also known as a token of peace, smoky quartz absorbs negative energy and keeps you safe.

You can also make this a spell bottle you can wear, leave in your car, or keep in your suitcase. Just grab a small bottle (can be picked up at any craft store or online), add in a small amount of coffee grounds and nutmeg, and replace the maple syrup with ground cayenne pepper (for road opening and getting over obstacles) and some smoky quartz chips. Say the spell and keep it on you when you travel.

LET IT BURN

A transformation spell to burn it all away (safely)

Sometimes, we all get the urge to burn it down, to burn our lives to the ground, put our past up in smoke, and start all over again. While we can't do that, for a variety of reasons, we can still honor our need to burn what we want to get rid of and start over, even in a small way. This spell will help you light up your life (and coffee) and get ready for a fresh start.

WITCH'S SAFETY WARNING: In this spell, we will be working with fire. As always, please be very careful around flames and practice fire safety at all times. This spell will also be working with alcohol, so if you're not of legal drinking age, skip this spell for now.

---

two small bowls

2 tablespoons lemon juice (*purification, happiness, openness, removing hexes, clarity, sun magic*)

2 tablespoons packed brown sugar (*overcoming enemies*)

a heat-resistant wineglass

2 ounces of rum (*ritual offering*)

a long lighter

⅛ teaspoon ground cinnamon (*luck, success, energy, happiness, psychic boost, healing, protection, fire energy*)

⅛ teaspoon ground nutmeg (*luck, lucid dreaming, attraction, psychic visions*)

⅛ teaspoon ground cloves (*protection, abundance, banishing negativity, courage, warmth*)

2 ounces amaretto (*open mind, warding against negativity, luck*)

2 cups strong-brewed medium roast coffee, lukewarm (*balance, flexibility, strength, reliability, grounding, determination*)

———————— ⁕ ————————

HOW TO CONJURE

STEP 1: Pour your lemon juice into one of the two bowls and add your brown sugar to the other bowl. Dip the rim of your wineglass into the lemon juice, then into the sugar. You have to do this quickly while the rim is still wet from the lemon juice.

STEP 2: Pour the rum into your wineglass. Slowly, cautiously, tilt the glass at a 45-degree angle. Get out your lighter. Before you ignite your lighter, say: "With this, I shall burn away the past and light my life anew. May the bridges I burn light the way."

STEP 3: Carefully, light the rum on fire. Make sure you keep it away from your face and hair. Return the glass back into the upright position and place it on a flat surface away from anything flammable. Turn off your lighter, if you haven't already, but do not extinguish the flame in the glass.

STEP 4: With your hand flat down on the table, hold the wineglass stem firmly between your index and middle finger and move your hand in a circular motion. This will swirl the flame in the glass to caramelize the sugar. Do this very carefully; don't swirl too hard or too fast.

STEP 5: When most of the sugar has been caramelized, stop swirling. Sprinkle the ground cinnamon, nutmeg, and cloves into the drink while saying: "Change is the spice of life. Like the phoenix, I'm ready to start this new cycle of life." The spices will cause visual sparks when added to the fire so do not be alarmed when this happens.

STEP 6: Quickly and carefully pour your amaretto over the rum, then add in your coffee. When you add in your coffee say: "With this, I leave my past behind and welcome the new me."

STEP 7: When the fire is out, the potion is ready to drink. Be careful, it'll still be very hot. As you drink, feel the fire and passion in your own heart melting away the past as you start something new.

FOR A DASH OF MAGIC...

- For best results, cast this during the new moon, as it will cleanse away the past and help you start over.
- When you drink this, write out everything you are planning to change in your life using coffee ink from "Let Me Spell It Out for You" on page 129.
- This is a great spell to perform at a coven meeting because of how visual it is.

SHAKE A LITTLE LOVE
A caffeinated love jar spell

Looking for love in the modern world can really be a nightmare for most witches. The endless scrolling through dating apps, getting ghosted more times than a haunted house, and trying to meet people who bewitch your heart rather make you feel hexed. While the dating scene is hell, here's a handy spell jar that will *hopefully* clear a path to true love. Or at least a second date.

---

a large glass jar with an airtight lid

paper and pen

an apple with seeds (*love, gratitude, abundance*)

⅓ cup coffee beans

2 tablespoons granulated sugar (*attraction, love, manifesting*)

⅓ cup fresh or dried rose petals (*love, compassion, protection*)

2 pieces star anise (*luck, happiness, protection, falling in love*)

HOW TO CONJURE

STEP 1: Pick up your glass jar and clean it (consider using the cleansing spray from the "Coffee Bar Altar" ritual on page 92). You want to make sure that the jar has a very tight lid so nothing can get in.

STEP 2: Take your paper and pen, and on one side of the paper, write out all of the qualities you wish to find in a romantic partner. Are they funny? Are they kind to animals? What does their five-year plan look like? You can be as detailed as you like, but don't get too specific or it can actually work against you. Remember, only add what is truly important to you: values, ethics, passions, stuff like that.

STEP 3: Turn your sheet of paper over and write down everything that's great about YOU (yes, there are great things about you, I promise). Write down every single thing you bring to the table. Are you empathic? Do you make the best vegan chocolate cake ever? Are you creative? Think of this as your dating profile to the universe. You've told the universe what you're looking for and let the universe know why you're the best match.

STEP 4: When you've finished, eat your apple. Read over your list one more time and see if there's anything you wish to change or add. Save the apple seeds.

STEP 5: When you're ready, take your paper and fold it half. Fold it in half two more times. Seal it with a kiss and place at the bottom of your jar.

STEP 6: Add in your coffee beans, sugar, rose petals, and apple seeds. Add in your two pieces of star anise—these represent you and you lover. If you are in or looking to be in a polyamorous relationship, add more star anise for the number of partners you desire.

STEP 7: Hold the jar in front of you and say, either out loud or in your mind: "I am opening myself up for a love that is right for me. I'm ready to find the match that is made for me. My heart is open and ready. Every time I shake this jar, love moves a little closer to me. For my highest good."

STEP 8: Put the lid on the jar tightly. Shake the jar once a day to release its powers and shake before going on a first date or scrolling through new dating profiles.

FOR A DASH OF MAGIC...

❋ If you want to seal your paper with a kiss, wear red lipstick for love and passion. You can also use a red wax seal on your paper to really seal the deal.

❋ Add a piece of rose quartz to the jar to increase that loving and romantic energy.

❋ While this spell is written for romantic love, you can use it for whatever type of love you wish to bring into your life, including a best friend.

❋ Add ingredients that represent the traits you want in a partner. If you want a partner who is very courageous and wise and knows where they're going in life, add in some cardamom pods. Looking for someone good with money? Add cloves. If you're looking for someone who is creative, compassionate, and a little witchy, add some hazelnuts. It's your jar!

❋ For best results, perform this spell on a Friday. Friday is ruled by Venus, the planet of love, giving love spells an extra boost.

❋ For best results, perform this during a waxing crescent moon, as it helps with manifesting and attraction.

❋ After casting this spell, do the "Fortune in Your Cup" ritual on page 99 to see what the future has planned for your love life.

❋ After casting this spell, drink a flat white coffee or the "You Mocha Me Crazy" brew on page 75 to help attract more love.

OH FRAPPÉ DAY

A spell for connecting to the world around you

In our modern world, it can be a struggle to take time out to enjoy the little things. A beautiful sunrise, a warm summer day, and just enjoying the sweetness of life. In this meditative spell, we'll be brewing up a traditional Greek frappé to help us connect with the universe and indulge in the little luxuries that life gives us. This will be a little different from the big coffee chain frappés you may be used to, but it'll taste just as good.

---

a drink shaker, jar, or blender

1 cup cold water

1 teaspoon instant coffee

2 teaspoons granulated sugar *(optional but recommended for multiplying the positive vibes)*

a tall glass

ice cubes

2 tablespoons milk *(optional for good vibes)*

2 teaspoons caramel *(positivity, comfort, transformation, soothing)*

a straw

HOW TO CONJURE

STEP 1: In your cocktail shaker or blender, add in 3 tablespoons water, your instant coffee, and sugar if you're using it. If you don't have a shaker or blender, use a jar with a very tight-fitting lid.

STEP 2: Shake or blend until the mixture turns into foam. As the mixture blends, think of all the good times you appreciate about your life, or even just things you're grateful about today.

STEP 3: When your mixture turns to foam, take your glass and add in your ice cubes. Pour in your mixture and add in your remaining water and the milk if you prefer.

STEP 4: Take your caramel and pour in a circular motion. As you pour, say: "Happy days are here to stay. I choose to celebrate the joys in life, in whatever way they choose to manifest. I connect with my highest good with every sip."

STEP 5: With your straw, stir your frappé together clockwise at least three times—this will attract the good vibes to you.

STEP 6: Sip and feel that connection to the world around you.

FOR A DASH OF MAGIC...

* Frappés are also associated with wealth, so you can easily turn this into a money spell by replacing caramel with the apple syrup from the "Piece of the Pie" brew on page 60.

* For best results, perform this spell during the full moon for gratitude and celebration of the wonders life has to offer you.

* For best results, cast this spell on a Sunday. Sunday is ruled by the sun, which is beneficial for abundance and happiness spells.

MAY YOUR CUP RUNNETH OVER
A spell for overwhelming blessings

The struggle is real for the modern witch. It seems like every day we're playing the game of life on hard mode and feeling lost, helpless, and even a little desperate. If you're looking for a little magical help to ease the load and give you an uplifting boost, here's the spell for you. While it won't fix everything in your life (you'll have to do that heavy lifting), it will help you open up to blessings that could fill your cup—both metaphorically and literally.

---

a coffee dripper

a small coffee cup or teacup with a large open rim

towels

1 large coffee filter

3 tablespoons medium roast coffee (*prosperity and reliability*)

3 teaspoons brown sugar (*multiplying*)

3 cups hot water (*sun water preferred for positivity*)

spoon

HOW TO BREW

STEP 1: Place your coffee dripper over your cup. Make sure that you have a lot of paper towels or regular tea towels under your cup as things will get messy. Put your coffee filter inside of your dripper. If you don't have a coffee dripper, get a bigger coffee mug, and place your filter over the cup, using binder clips to keep the filter in place.

STEP 2: Add your coffee grounds to the filter. As you add in your coffee say, either out loud or in your mind: "With this coffee, I am opening my heart to the flow of good vibes. Any blessings that the universe has to offer, I shall receive. For my highest good."

STEP 3: Add in your sugar, one teaspoon at a time. When you add in your first teaspoon, say: "I multiply this blessing onefold." With the second teaspoon, say: "I multiply this blessing twofold." With the third teaspoon, say: "I multiply this blessing threefold."

STEP 4: Heat up your water in either a kettle, single-cup coffee maker, or microwave. You may not use all the water, but you want more water than you need to overfill your coffee mug. Make sure the water is warm but not overly hot for your safety.

STEP 5: Pour your water into your dripper, clockwise. As you pour, speak the blessing you wish to receive out loud. For example, if you're looking for a blessing to come to you in the form of money, say: "I ask the universe to pour an abundance of money into my cup of life that will sustain me and help me grow the life I desire." If you're looking for a blessing to come to you in the form of wellness, say: "I ask the universe to pour good physical, mental, and spiritual health into my cup of life to help me grow strong and enjoy life to the fullest." Whatever you need.

STEP 6: Continue to pour until the cup is overflowing and the water is running over the sides of the cup.

STEP 7: Stop pouring and put your water to the side. Wait for the water to finish dripping before taking your cup slowly and carefully in your hands, and say: "My cup will fill me with everything I need and then some. For my highest good."

STEP 8: Drink and enjoy.

FOR A DASH OF MAGIC...

- Draw a sigil of abundance, blessings, or happiness on your coffee filter before putting it in your coffee dripper or cup. (See "Sigil Magic" on page 144.)

- For best results, cast this spell during the waxing crescent moon for manifesting, attracting good things, and building prosperity.

- Use the ingredients from the "Everything Is Golden" potion on page 69 to help you create opportunities for blessings.

- If you're using this spell to bring money into your life, use the ingredients from the "Piece of the Pie" potion on page 60 for extra money magic.

- If you're using this spell to bring health into your life, use the ingredients from the "Brew Me Back to Life" potion on page 73 for extra health magic.

- If you're using this spell to bring magic and love (and a little lust) into your life, use the ingredients from the "Devil's Brew" potion on page 58 for an extra boost of all those qualities.

- Before drinking your coffee, perform the "Are You Seer-ing This?" scrying ritual on page 111 to see how these blessing may manifest into your life.

DROWN MY SORROWS IN CHOCOLATE

A spell to bake away bad vibes and enchant your feelings

Who doesn't love a good coffee with a yummy baked treat? Much like making a cup of coffee, baking is a great form of spell casting, as it can be a meditative practice to help you clear your mind while infusing your personal magic to make your spells come alive. In this spell, we'll be reimagining both the brownie and the sundae with a more adult theme by creating an affogato. While this is still an indulgent dessert, making it can soothe hurt feelings, ease your soul, and enchant good vibes by increasing your energy. Not even the most vengeful witch can be mad while eating this.

FOR BAKING
oven
mixing bowl
9 x 13-inch baking pan
parchment paper
a large spoon or spatula
a small bowl

a spoon

FOR THE BROWNIES
2 sticks of butter (*increasing tenacity, easing change, increasing spiritual connection, soothing energy*)

2 cups granulated sugar *(attraction, smoothing things over, manifesting)*

⅓ cup espresso powder *(energy, clarity, protection, banishments, awareness, speed, productivity, and breaking curses)*

4 eggs *(new life, happiness, wishes)*

1½ cups all-purpose flour

1 cup unsweetened cocoa powder *(self-love, replenished magical energy, nurturing, grounding, balance, increased emotional energy)*

FOR THE AFFOGATO FINISH
1 tablespoon fudge ice cream topping

1 ounce espresso

1 to 2 scoops of coffee ice cream *(grounding, cleansing, removing energy blocks, clarity, motivation, happiness)*

2 tablespoons chocolate-covered coffee beans *(optional)*

HOW TO CONJURE

STEP 1: Preheat your oven to 350°F. Melt your butter either on the stovetop or microwave. Allow to cool completely.

STEP 2: When the butter is cool, mix the melted butter and sugar together in a bowl. As you stir, visualize your negative feelings: your hurt, your doubt, your anger, and watch them melt away.

STEP 3: Add in your espresso powder and mix until just combined. As you stir, visualize banishing the negativity and giving a boost to all the good things you wish to feel: happiness, peace, love, joy, etc.

STEP 4: Add in the eggs and stir until combined. Then add your flour and cocoa powder.

STEP 5: Stir this mixture together. As you stir, say, either out loud or in your mind: "Let me bake better feelings into my heart and mind. As of this moment, my pain has now ended, and the love and joy can now begin. I deserve to feel good. For my highest good."

STEP 6: When you finish stirring, line your 9 x 13-inch baking pan with parchment paper and transfer your batter into the pan using your spoon. Bake for 30 minutes.

STEP 7: When the brownies are done, take them out of the oven and let them cool. While the brownies cool, heat up your fudge and brew your espresso.

STEP 8: When the brownies have cooled, cut off a piece and put it into your small bowl. Take a scoop or two of the coffee ice cream and place on top of the brownie and add the fudge. Take your espresso and pour on top of your brownie and ice cream. As you pour, say: "I melt away all that no longer serves me, leaving only the sweetness that life has to give."

STEP 9: Sprinkle on the chocolate-covered coffee beans and enjoy.

MAGIC TRICK

When baking with chocolate (chocolate cake, brownies, double-chocolate cookies, etc.) replace the water with brewed coffee. It won't make your treat taste like coffee, but it will enhance the chocolate flavor while adding the magic of coffee. If you want to add coffee flavor to your dessert, add in some instant coffee or instant espresso.

FOR A DASH OF MAGIC...

☀ Add in a teaspoon of hazelnut syrup, spread, or extract to your brownie batter for an increase of witchcraft.

☀ This is a great dessert to make and give to someone to smooth things over and mend things up after a rough patch, especially if you're the one who's wronged someone.

☀ Draw a sigil in the brownie batter for what you wish to evoke in the brownie: happiness, love, peace of mind, etc.

☀ Replace the coffee ice cream with vanilla ice cream for inner peace, comfort, and healing.

☀ To set the mood, light a coffee candle from the "A Cup Full of Light" ritual on page 132 to help you meditate and relax while you enjoy your dessert spell.

☀ For best results, cast this spell during the waning crescent moon for meditation and self-care.

GET THE HEX OUT

A spell for banishing someone from your life

Not all relationships last forever. What once was a magical connection has turned sour, and it's time to cut the ties that bind. If you've tried everything else, this spell may help you get rid of this person from your life and keep them out for good.

½ teaspoon ground cayenne pepper *(removing obstacles, speeding things up, cleansing, protection, strength, courage, creating hexes)*

½ teaspoon ground cloves *(protection, banishment)*

a small bowl

3 tablespoons used coffee grounds *(either grounds from coffee they drank or their favorite kind of ground coffee)*

a piece of string

scissors

your cell phone

HOW TO CONJURE

STEP 1: Gather your cayenne and cloves and put them in a small bowl. Set aside for now.

STEP 2: Invite the person you wish to banish from your life over for coffee. Give them one more chance to see if you can end things amicably. If you cannot or simply want them out of your life, ask them to leave your home, and your life. When they leave, take the grounds from the coffee you made and put them into the cayenne-and-cloves mixture.

WITCH'S SAFETY TIP: This step is only for the people in your life who you want to banish but are nonviolent—someone you think you could reason with if given the opportunity. If you're trying to banish a person who has been violent in any way or someone you feel unsafe around, do not meet with them alone and do not meet with them in your home. Even if you feel a little sketched out by them, do not let them in. In cases where you cannot or should not meet with the person, do this instead: if you know what coffee they like, brew that, throw the brewed coffee out, and put those grounds into the mixture.

STEP 3: Mix the cayenne, cloves, and coffee grounds together in your bowl counterclockwise three times. As you stir, think of a wall being built around your home and around yourself. Picture your door being boarded up, and the person who's causing you grief being as far away from you as possible.

STEP 4: Take your string with two hands and hold it over the mixture. Say: "This is where our connection ends. Our ties no longer bind. I release you from my life, and from this day forth, you will never set another foot through my door. For my highest good."

STEP 5: Cut the string and put the two pieces in the mixture.

STEP 6: Take the mixture outside and bury it in your front yard, as near to your front door as possible. You can also sprinkle the mixture around your doorstep. If you don't have a front yard, throw the mixture in the garbage and immediately take out the trash.

STEP 7: Block that person and their number from everything—your contacts, all apps, email, etc.

FOR A DASH OF MAGIC...

* For best results, cast this spell during the waning gibbous moon, as it is associated with cleansing and exile spells.

* Add a little bit of espresso to your mix for speed, banishment, and curse casting.

* For best results, cast this spell on a Saturday, as it is ruled over by the planet Saturn and is optimal for banishment spells.

* Cast a salt circle around your door and sprinkle salt on the windowsills for extra protection.

* If you are dealing with a legal matter concerning the person you're trying to banish, add ½ teaspoon of nutmeg to the mix as nutmeg brings legal justice. By adding this, your legal matter with this person will settle swiftly and in your favor.

* Brew and drink the "Coffee Protect Me" potion on page 89 for an extra safety measure.

* Write a protection sigil on a rock and bury it with your mixture or keep it near your door for extra protection.

* Mix some of the coffee grounds from the "Let's Speed Things Along" spell on page 152 to make this banishment happen more quickly.

* Perform a variation of the "One Last Cup" ritual on page 122. However, instead of using it as a tribute, air out all your grievances at the altar, as if you were talking to them. Get everything you need to say off your chest. Then, get rid of the altar and their coffee grounds.

MONEY FOLLOWS WHEREVER I GO
A caffeinated money spell

This witch doesn't recommend that you spend your precious time on this earth chasing the almighty dollar, but living in modern times means living under capitalism, which means you do need to have access to some funds in order to have a livable life. If you're looking for cash to flow to you effortlessly, mix up this coffee powder and keep it with you, so money is always flowing toward you.

NOTE: Despite wild claims from witches and "spiritual coaches" on social media, there is so spell, potion, or ritual you can do to make a million dollars overnight (unless you're like a *really* powerful witch). This spell is not intended to get you into a higher tax bracket quickly. This is merely to help money flow to you continually, especially when you need it. However, don't use it to solve all your financial problems.

---

1 tablespoon medium roast coffee grounds
(prosperity, reliability, speeding things along, removing blocks)

2 teaspoons dried lavender *(relaxation,*
peace, getting things without a struggle)

1 tablespoon dried ginger *(quick manifestation, confidence,*
energy boost, inner power, abundance, balance, success)

2 teaspoons dried peppermint *(positive*
thoughts, luck, prosperity, protection)

a coffee grinder or mortar and pestle

a jar, sachet, or ziplock bag

a few coins *(any kind)*

a pyrite crystal *(optional, associated with money)*

———————— ❖ ————————

HOW TO CONJURE

STEP 1: Add your coffee grounds, lavender, ginger, and peppermint together in your coffee grinder. If you prefer to do things a little witchier, use a mortar and pestle.

STEP 2: Blend those herbs together using your preferred method. As you do this, say, either out loud or in your head: "Money, money, money, you will always come to me. You flow to me easily whenever I am in need. Money, money, money, in whatever form you may be. You always know where to find me and keep me in the green. For my highest good."

STEP 3: When you have finished mixing the herbs, pour them in a jar, sachet, or ziplock bag—whatever you prefer. Add in your coins. If you have pyrite, put it in there now.

STEP 4: Place your jar or bag wherever you need it the most. It can be at your office, in your purse, or at the kitchen table where you usually pay your bills. It can be in the cash register at your work. You can even put it in a smaller jar charm and keep it around your neck when you're at work. The point is to keep it as close to money as possible.

STEP 5: Get that money.

FOR A DASH OF MAGIC...

* Keep this at your "Coffee Bar Altar" (page 92) so that you are starting the day by looking at it, getting you into the money mindset.

* For best results, cast this spell on a Thursday, as it is ruled by Jupiter and favors money and business spells.

* For best results, charge this mixture under a full moon to bring it to its full manifesting power.

* Hold this mixture in your hands while drinking the "Piece of the Pie" potion on page 60 for a boost of abundance. You can even use the coffee grounds from that potion and add them into this mixture—just make sure they are dried out first.

* Draw a money or abundance sigil on the jar or a piece of paper and place it in the jar or sachet for an extra boost of money. Make sure you write it in green ink, as green represents abundance and prosperity.

* If you are in a creative business, add a few hazelnuts into your mixture before grinding the mixture, as hazelnuts are associated with creativity.

* Pour the mixture in your coffee Zen garden ("A Moment to Get Grounded," page 127) to keep at work so you can have it close to you.

* Put this mixture in a small packet and place it in the bag you use during the "It's in the Bag" ritual on page 124 to manifest money.

ONE LAST DASH OF MAGIC

◦ ◦ ☽ ✳ ☾ ◦ ◦

Well, we've reached the end of our journey, witches. However, just because our cup of coffee is empty doesn't mean that your coffee magic adventures are over. In fact, you're now ready to brew up some magic of your own. I hope this book has helped you appreciate the magic of coffee. Not just its powers to help you get through the day, but to appreciate its rich history, full flavor, and enchanted spirit that is brewed with each cup. I hope you learn to savor your morning coffee ritual and find ways to add your own magic to your coffee shop order. Don't be afraid to make sigils in your latte art or read your future in your coffee grounds. Experimenting with new things is what makes life fun. Magic isn't only found at the bottom of your coffee mug but in every area of your life. So, get out there and face the world, one caffeinated brew at a time.

Remember, you are magic.

RESOURCES

Chapa, Asia Lu. *The Home Café: Creative Recipes for Espresso, Matcha, Tea, and Coffee Drinks*. Salem, MA: Page Street Publishing, 2022.

Colonna-Dashwood, Maxwell. *Coffee Dictionary: An A–Z of Coffee, from Growing and Roasting to Brewing and Tasting*. London: Mitchell Beazley, 2017.

Hoffmann, James. *How to Make the Best Coffee at Home*. London: Mitchell Beazley, 2022.

Illes, Judika. *Encyclopedia of 5,000 Spells*. San Francisco, CA: HarperOne, 2009.

Murphy-Hiscock, Arin. *The Witch's Book of Self-Care*. Avon, MA: Adams Media, 2018.

Vanderbeck, Paige. *Green Witchcraft: A Practical Guide to Discovering the Magic of Plants, Herbs, Crystals, and Beyond*. Berkeley, CA: Rockridge Press, 2020.

Wigington, Patti. *Herb Magic: An Introduction to Magical Herbalism and Spells*. Berkeley, CA: Rockridge Press, 2020.

Wild, Elsie. *Herbal Tea Magic for the Modern Witch*. Berkeley, CA: Ulysses Press, 2021.

ABOUT THE AUTHOR

Elsie Wild is a writer and witch haunting the Adirondack Mountains of Upstate New York. A lifelong student of divination, Wild has been a practitioner of tarot, astrology, numerology, and herbalism for over a decade and has written horoscopes, articles, and guides for various publications. She is the author of *Herbal Tea Magic for the Modern Witch* (Ulysses Press, 2021), *The Secrets of Fortune Telling*, *The Secrets of Spiritual Healing*, *The Little Book of Chakras*, and *The Magic Art of Fortune Telling*, an oracle deck. When she is not writing or casting spells, Wild is arguing with her tarot cards and making terrible puns.